T0010933

WHAT WOULD JURGEN KLOPP DO?

WHAT WOULD JURGEN KLOPP DO?

LIFE LESSONS FROM A CHAMPION

TOM VICTOR

SEVEN DIALS

First published in Great Britain in 2020 by Seven Dials
This paperback edition published in 2022 by Seven Dials,
an imprint of The Orion Publishing Group Ltd
Carmelite House, 50 Victoria Embankment
London EC4Y 0DZ

An Hachette UK Company

3 5 7 9 10 8 6 4

Text by Tom Victor

All rights reserved. No part of this publication may be
reproduced, stored in a retrieval system, or transmitted
in any form or by any means, electronic, mechanical,
photocopying, recording, or otherwise, without the
prior permission of both the copyright owner and
the above publisher of this book.

A CIP catalogue record for this book is
available from the British Library.

ISBN (Mass Market Paperback) 978 1 8418 8415 8
ISBN (eBook) 978 1 8418 8416 5

Printed and bound in Great Britian by Clays Ltd, Elcograf, S.p.A

www.orionbooks.co.uk

Dedicated to **Brendan Rodgers,**
for drawing with Everton and
making this all possible.

CONTENTS

⚽ ⚽ ⚽

INTRODUCTION

A few years ago, if someone had told you that you should be more like a great football manager, it would have sounded odd. Managers were the people you respected for their achievements or held in high regard for how they transformed the club you supported. They were not people you wanted to see as role models or take life advice from. Or at least they weren't – until Jurgen Klopp.

We all remember where we were when Jurgen Klopp first appeared on our radar. For many of us, myself included, it was when he was in charge of Borussia Dortmund. We cared about Dortmund because we cared about him, and they stood out because, well, it was impossible not to notice Jurgen Klopp, even back then. At the time, Dortmund were everything a European football club should be. And everything a lot of English clubs were not (or at least that's how it felt). Dortmund had loyal fans who got up for every game, home or away; they felt a real connection with their city. Their team was made up of young, hungry players. And, of course, they had a manager who reflected all those great things in his own behaviour.

Jurgen came to the forefront at a time when it was easy to have fallen out of love with football. I was a little exhausted by it all myself. The 2010s were when European football was beginning to get a little stale. Crowds were getting older and more bitter. The same handful of clubs were gaining a stranglehold on the game. Even international football was starting to lose its bite after an underwhelming World Cup at the beginning of the decade. But then along came Jurgen Klopp. It turns out he was just what the game – and what we, the fans – needed.

Perhaps you were only vaguely aware of him back then. Or perhaps you're loudly tsking, remembering how you followed his career in Mainz before he even *started* at Dortmund. It's OK either way. Plenty of football fans *knew about* Klopp when he was in Germany, but they only really *knew* him when he arrived in

England. You could enjoy his charisma and his sound-bites from afar, but when he took over at Liverpool FC in 2015 it became clear it wasn't just for show: this was him, through and through.

Klopp is the cool uncle of football. He's your school friend's dad who always greets you like you're *his* friend as well. The popular colleague who always makes you feel like you're on his level. The hugs he gave, for example, weren't just special treatment saved for the big TV games: they were for every game. The infectious laugh wasn't a man playing up to the cameras: that was just how he laughed. The eccentric soundbites? That was just how he expressed himself. And the more I've found out about Jurgen Klopp since he joined Liverpool FC, the more I've found to like about him.

And he has time to do all of this while still being great at all the things a football manager has to excel at.

Klopp's Dortmund team stopped the all-conquering Bayern Munich – twice! – and as Liverpool manager he won the Champions League in the superclub era without a superclub. That's harder than you might think. If he wasn't so successful at his job, maybe we wouldn't hear so much about him, but here's the thing: his character and success go hand in hand. He is, for example, a great motivator, but he achieves this in a way that someone without his larger-than-life personality couldn't. His character coupled with his skill is a winning combination, and one that is completely unique to him.

When someone achieves so much, you might expect fans of rival teams to hate them, but it's impossible to hate Jurgen Klopp. His Liverpool predecessor Brendan Rodgers even let Klopp move into his old house on Merseyside, saying, 'Whatever help he needed as a manager, I was there for that.'[1] The best you can muster is jealousy, but soon enough you realise life's too short for even that. So, from family and friendship to food, film and a great deal more, this is your guide to all of life's challenges inspired by the Liverpool living legend.

It's time to ask, therefore, not what Jurgen Klopp can do for you, but what *you* can do to be more like Jurgen Klopp.

'There needs to be one plan, one voice, one belief. It will not always be perfect, because we are not perfect, but it is our way'

JURGEN KLOPP[2]

1. THE MOST IMPORTANT THING

⚽ ⚽ ⚽

JURGEN KLOPP AND FAMILY

Kicking off with family is an absolute no-brainer. Life begins with family – quite literally, of course, with those nine months spent inside your mother's womb – and it's no coincidence that nine months is the amount of time that passed between Jurgen Klopp's Liverpool starting their 2018–19 Champions League campaign and them lifting the trophy in Madrid.

OK, fine, maybe it is a bit of a coincidence, but the point still stands. Family isn't just the first thing you'll encounter in your life, it's also the most important.

Baz Luhrmann reminded us of this in the song 'Everybody's Free (To Wear Sunscreen)', and Jurgen Klopp has recognised it by cultivating relationships in football that are far more 'father and son' than 'boss and employee'.

Most football managers deal in formations, philosophies or both. It helps define their greatest teams, and it helps define them as people. Jurgen Klopp isn't like most football managers – he does family trees.[*]

When you think about great football managers and the great teams they've built, you can mentally map out the players on the pitch as if they're an extension of the managers themselves. With Pep Guardiola, you see the 4-3-3 of his great Barcelona teams and their devastating tiki-taka football. Antonio Conte had his 3-5-2 at Chelsea, a set-up that he also used in Euro 2016 to beat European champions Spain with his Italy team. Jurgen Klopp has formations that work for him, sure, but his strategy goes beyond that. He thinks of the personal connections first – everything else is in place simply to allow those connections to flourish and his players to express themselves.

---

[*] OK, he also does formations *a bit*, I guess, but bear with me.

BRING OTHERS UP WITH YOU

If you're working with Jurgen Klopp, you're part of the family. He hands down old secrets like heirlooms, building you in his image. It works, too, leading you to follow his path so closely that you don't even notice until it's too late to turn back without feeling like you've disappointed him somehow. He has shown us how close relationships aren't a means to an end or something to be perfected. Instead, if you approach them with honesty and warmth then you'll still end up with the best possible outcome. You don't treat your family well because you think you'll get something out of it in return – you do it because *it's the right thing to do*.

It works for both sides, too. When you play under Jurgen Klopp, you're not just part of the team – you're part of the family. It's not like other clubs, where you're just passing through on your way from point A to point B. Instead, you form lasting relationships. Why do you think so many Klopp acolytes followed him to other clubs, or went on to play for David Wagner or Daniel Farke, fellow members of the Dortmund family?

You probably know why, too. Positivity is infectious, and there's no positivity quite like the positivity you get when you surround yourself with people like Jurgen Klopp.

The classic example is David Wagner. Wagner was born in Germany but played international football for the United States, making him the perfect accompaniment to Klopp – the French fries to Klopp's bratwurst, if you will (if you came here for the piping-hot German sausage content, you're in luck – you'll get to the food and drink section on page 117, just be patient): their background was similar, but the American experience – the land of Klopp's musical idols Kiss (more on his music tastes later) and a country still developing its own footballing identity – added another dimension.

Wagner was like the prodigal son, who Klopp had never forgotten after their years playing together at Mainz in the early 1990s. Wagner described the relationship as 'more like [having] a family member than a friend'.[1] He was best man at Klopp's wedding and in 2011 he took charge of Borussia Dortmund's second team while Klopp himself coached the seniors. Klopp helped Wagner in management, sure, but as with all Klopp relationships, the benefits went both ways. It was like a CEO training his son to take over the family business, even if, as it turned out, Wagner would go his own way by managing Huddersfield and Schalke.

Hari Sethi, a lifelong Red and podcast host for Anfield Index Pro, sums it up perfectly when he says, 'The key word here would be empowerment.'

When I spoke to him about Klopp's unique way of engendering a family atmosphere in his team, he shared that, 'Klopp appears to have relatively little ego, seems generally happy to admit when he's made a mistake or delegate tasks when he feels others know better. He's also happy to share knowledge with others, rather than regarding his tactical knowledge or experience as exclusive secrets to keep hold of.

'[Assistant coach] Pep Lijnders has also spoken at length on how he's consistently been empowered by Klopp to take on more and more responsibility and feel comfortable with challenging the manager when he feels it's necessary; it's a collaborative environment rather than the traditional English model where the manager wields an unhealthy amount of power.'

All of this serves as a reminder that the cornerstone to a great family relationship is teamwork. There are things you'll be able to teach your kids, such as how to shave or ride a bike, and things they can teach you, like how to post to an Instagram story. There's so much you can learn from your family and empowering those around you really is better for everyone.

Q: Your teenage son fancies a girl in his class but doesn't know how to go about asking her out on a date – WWJKD?

A: Jurgen Klopp pep-talks aren't like regular pep-talks. He'll tell you to be yourself, but he'll make you think you reached that decision all by yourself. Expect a long, rambling speech about how a relationship is a lot like a pop song. The best bits are those that come to you spontaneously, when you're in the shower or just about to nod off. What does it all mean? Nothing. But also everything.

PASS DOWN LIFE LESSONS

You're probably wondering how you can take these lessons and apply them to your own family life. While some of it might *sound* a little alien, don't worry – I've got your back.

When you're part of Klopp's football family, it teaches you some lessons. The first, and most important one, is that you don't absolutely *need* to be as good as Jurgen himself. If everyone with a famous family member held themselves to those ridiculously high standards and gave up out of fear of not meeting them, the world would look very different. Frank Lampard Junior would never have earned a move to Chelsea. Nancy Sinatra would never have recorded 'These Boots Are Made for Walking'. Simba would never have defeated Scar.

When you look at your own family members, you need to see two things: people you love deeply and would do anything for, sure, but also people who you can periodically mock and one-up from a place of affection. Across the footballing spectrum, managers have worked with their sons, fighting off shouts of nepotism from a distance, but Klopp treats all his favourite players like his blood. There's the emotional praise, characterised by those hugs. But there's also the sense that, on those occasions his charges make a mistake, he's there to get them back on the horse. He's not angry, he's just disappointed.

'Jurgen does really care about the squad and his staff. Players will understand and absorb more of our philosophy when they feel how much we care about them'

PEP LIJNDERS[2]

THE KLOPP FAMILY TREE

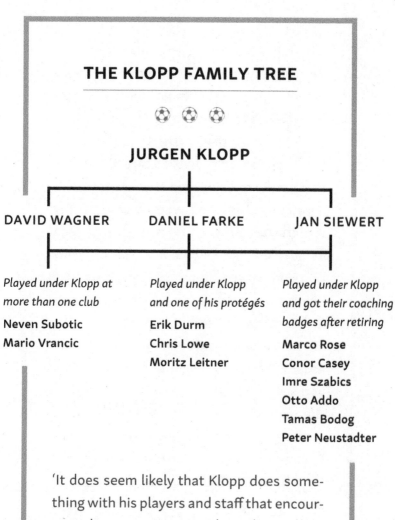

⚽ ⚽ ⚽

JURGEN KLOPP

DAVID WAGNER

Played under Klopp at more than one club

Neven Subotic
Mario Vrancic

DANIEL FARKE

Played under Klopp and one of his protégés

Erik Durm
Chris Lowe
Moritz Leitner

JAN SIEWERT

Played under Klopp and got their coaching badges after retiring

Marco Rose
Conor Casey
Imre Szabics
Otto Addo
Tamas Bodog
Peter Neustadter

'It does seem likely that Klopp does something with his players and staff that encourages them to go into coaching themselves, whether it's encouraging them to think more deeply about football or simply creating a happy dressing room,' football writer Huw Davies tells me.

Klopp has that fatherly aura about him, the dad who doesn't care when he's being embarrassing, and even leans into it. If you're a dad who's worried about being too cringeworthy, or fears not being seen as 'cool' enough for your kids, there's really no need. Jurgen Klopp has shown us how being cringeworthy is *part of* being a great father figure, not something to avoid.

The mystique surrounding him isn't necessarily obvious to begin with, but the more you see of him around those close to him, the more you realise why they hold him in such high esteem. He's made mistakes, but who hasn't? It's about how you bounce back from those mistakes, and about making sure those who come after you can make new, fresh mistakes of their own.

Coached Dortmund II, now managers:

If you grew up with siblings, you'll have quickly become sick of being compared with them at every point in your life. It doesn't matter if your brother got better grades at school, or if your sister had more of a knack for music. I can tell you now that they were just as tired of hearing about you being the sporty one as you were of being told about their achievements, and as soon as you realised it was about complementing each other rather than competing, things improved dramatically. If you couldn't stop fighting with your siblings when you were growing up, but now get on much better, this is why.

Jurgen Klopp might be the common link between the managers who worked under him before flying the nest, but it would be wrong to think of them all as Klopp Mk II – they each have their own characteristics.

David Wagner is the sensible, strait-laced older brother. The right level of reserved, bringing balance to his managerial jobs. He's not active enough to be considered the main character, but he's the neutral, calm head who you definitely understand the value of when he's not there.

Daniel Farke is the eccentric middle child. He's too big a character to go through life unnoticed, and has too high an opinion of his own abilities to *want* to fade into the background. He likes being seen as his own man, but he has picked up more of Klopp's eccentricities than he might care to admit.

Jan Siewert is the baby, still finding his way in the world. The least developed of the trio, he's prone to taking his cue from others within his own generation, not just from the patriarch. There might be times where this makes him look meek or weak, but that doesn't mean he isn't still an important part of this story. 'It's a common misconception that Siewert was one of Klopp's protégés . . . the two never actually met before Huddersfield played Liverpool in the Premier League in 2019,' journalist and Liverpool fan Steven Chicken notes. 'It's interesting that his two actual employees have so far done better than Siewert, who merely came up in the same system Klopp left behind.'

Played under Klopp at more than one club:

Managers have their favourites, and you'll see plenty of players follow their boss from one club to the next. Maurizio Sarri has Gonzalo Higuain. Brendan Rodgers had Joe Allen. Gary Johnson had . . . his son Lee Johnson. When Jurgen Klopp left Mainz for

Borussia Dortmund, he took **Neven Subotic** and **Mario Vrancic** along with him. Did it work? Well, why don't you look at the trophy cabinet.

Played under Klopp *and* one of his protégés:

Every good family has its hand-me-downs, and the Klopp dynasty is no different. That Vrancic-shaped jumper might have been too small for Klopp at Liverpool, but it fitted Daniel Farke just fine; **Erik Durm** served his purpose for a few years, but after he'd been outgrown he was left to Wagner. **Chris Lowe** and **Moritz Leitner** weren't going to be left gathering dust in a corner when they could still be put to use. Sharing is caring, folks.

Played under Klopp and got their coaching badges after retiring as players:

The presence of Klopp protégés in football doesn't begin and end with the former Dortmund II coaches who broke free from the nest. Coaching as part of a Klopp machine is one route in, but *playing* under him is another. **Marco Rose, Conor Casey, Imre Szabics, Otto Addo, Tamas Bodog** and **Peter Neustadter** are just a few of those who earned their coaching badges after playing for the German, and it won't end there. You've probably got your own ideas about which members of his Liverpool squad will find their way into a dugout after retiring – I know I do.

In an interview with *The Athletic*, Klopp's Liverpool number two Pep Lijnders commented that, 'There is a saying that people don't care how much you know until they know how much you care. And I think every-one who works with Jurgen has the feeling he really cares about you and your devel-opment.'[3] Ultimately, Klopp's family tree shows that if you're all moving in the same direction, what benefits the unit will bene-fit the individual as well.

'There is no ego, he purely searches for the right thing to do'

PEP LIJNDERS[4]

KEEP IT REAL

Think about any conversation with your family when you go home for Christmas or a birthday. There might be mundane chats about what you've been up to at work ('Oh, is that really what you do?'), or dreadful questions about what's going on in your love life ('So, how's the dating scene nowadays?'), but, no matter how bad your mood or the amount of chocolate your grandmother has forced you to consume, you can normally swerve those with a couple of creative man-oeuvres. And, let's face it, the real reason why you're even bothering to respond to your family's next-level inquisition is because, like everyone else in the room, you yearn for each other's company.

When someone is as relatable as Jurgen Klopp, it isn't difficult to understand why you want to be in his company – you feel a connection with him. There's no huge stretch needed, unlike with those super-famous people who will seem 'just like' you and me before casually mentioning their multiple private jets or £500 bottles of champagne or something else to remind you that, no, actually, we'll never understand their lives.

You just sense that it would be different with

Klopp. Even if he has more money and fame than your average person, it's hard to imagine him doing things differently now compared to when he was a kid. He probably does the big shop at his local supermarket every week, even if he sometimes gets the 'Finest' bread or 'Taste the Difference' salami as a treat. He probably has the occasional beer in the same local as the fans, even if there are nights when he'd prefer the peace and quiet of dinner and drinks in the comfort of his own home. And he probably takes it *very* seriously.

THE KLOPPING LIST

Jurgen Klopp is a man who knows what he wants at all times. As the head of the family, you don't need to be sure of what you want to the point of ignoring everyone and everything else, but a sense of direction can't exactly hurt. It's not just about the big responsibilities and grand gestures, either – nothing is too small, even if you think it can't possibly matter. I still remember those mornings following my mum or dad around the supermarket, pointing out the items with bright packaging or a frighten-ingly high sugar content (let's face it, these were usually the same thing). If I'd had my way, Friday-night dinner would have been cheeseburgers with a chocolate chip cookie garnish, and I'd have been the first child in decades to contract scurvy in north-west London. The players Klopp has signed have arrived after a long pursuit, brought in to fill a very specific role, and you can generally see their impact right away. With that in mind, why would he restrict that focus to shopping for footballers?

Here's what we'd get with a Klopp shopping list in the real world, when he's tasked with heading down to the big Tesco for his football family.

- Wholemeal pasta, to give his players the energy for all that gegenpressing.
- Protein shakes, for recovery.
- Cheese, to help with those cheesy grins.
- Party poppers, because there's always time for an impromptu celebration.
- Sugar. Not too much, though – as the shop assistant tells him, 'You're sweet enough as it is.'
- Bluetooth speakers. As you'll find out in

the music section later on, Jurgen likes things loud.

- Four identical pairs of glasses. How else do you think he has them looking so clean all the time?
- Shot glasses. After all, you miss 100 per cent of the shots you don't take.
- French mushrooms, for the European champignons. Geddit?!
- A crate of the finest German beer. *Prost!*

'It's clear that he develops deep, almost familial bonds with his players and it shows with the levels of commitment he's able to foster among the group'

HARI SETHI

Q: You're playing basketball in the driveway with your 14-year-old son. He's been going through a growth spurt recently, and you're worried the extra reach will give him an advantage – WWJKD?

A: The first time a son beats his father at sports is a momentous occasion for both. It's a symbolic passing of the torch, and the way you react – on either side – will say a lot about you. You're a competitive person, though. You need to win, making it easy to gloat, or lose in a way that makes it look like you're not all that bothered by the result. This is difficult. The only solution is to compromise: start off slow, giving him a bit of a head-start and laughing it off. Big him up at every opportunity. Maybe even mention the whole passing of the torch thing, to give the impression you're being gracious in defeat even before you've actually lost. Then, as soon as he's let his guard down, you pounce.

Look, he'll have plenty of opportunity to beat you over the next few years, but you might never get this chance again. Didn't see that one coming, did you? Well, nor did he, which is what makes it the perfect ruse.

When you were at school, studying for exams, you might have found yourself wondering why your folks seemed to actively enjoy the concept of working. Turns out it wasn't that – it was the pride that came in the sharing of your achievements. When Jurgen Klopp sprints down the touchline after a dramatic late winner, he's celebrating the power of his own brand of love. And it doesn't stop there – whenever David Wagner or Daniel Farke lead their teams to victory, their mentor is up there smiling. You've seen that scene from *The Simpsons* where Lisa gets one last jam with her idol, saxophonist Bleeding Gums Murphy. Many people will wonder what the key to Klopp's management success is, but I reckon a large part is to do with how he creates and leads his own football family.

2. HUGS AND HANDSHAKES

❀ ❀ ❀

FRIENDSHIP WITH JURGEN KLOPP

If you're a football fan, you'll have at least one friend with whom you bonded over the beautiful game. That's not a 'probably' – it's a reality. Football is a great unifier. You can use it to make small talk with your sister's boyfriend, or as a tool to avoid talking politics with that one acquaintance who you suspect has some 'questionable' opinions about the world.

The sport is unique for another reason, too. When discussing some of your other interests – from film to music, TV to video games – a difference of opinion can set you apart from someone. With football, though, arguments can – and do – bring people closer together.

As a West Ham fan, I've argued for hours with my fellow supporters about both Kevin Nolan and Jeremy Corbyn, about Harry Redknapp and Boris Johnson, and in both cases only one of these debates brought me closer to the other person. For the Liverpool supporters in my life, it's much the same. I'll see arguments rage for days about Rafa Benitez's flaws and who was better out of Martin Skrtel and Daniel Agger, and the simple fact of caring that much about the club is the most important thing. At the heart of it, you're all on the same side.

It says a lot, then, that there's even one topic capable of uniting fans of Liverpool and plenty of supporters of other clubs. The sort of person who people don't have to lie about liking to fit in, because they've always had time for him. Still, part of the reason why Jurgen Klopp has that kind of power is that he himself has a great grasp of friendship.

'As a character he is a person who relates to the player'

NURI SAHIN, FORMER LIVERPOOL AND BORUSSIA DORTMUND MIDFIELDER[1]

THE POWER OF THE KLOPPELGANGER

There are two universal truths in life: 'a dog is man's best friend' and 'after a while, owners start to look just like their dogs'. Jurgen Klopp has recognised this – of course he has, he's a very perceptive man – and so he's done what any sensible manager would do: he's surrounded himself with people who could pass for Klopp himself in a poor disguise.

Within months of taking over at Liverpool, he hired Andreas Kornmayer as the club's fitness and conditioning coach. Is Kornmayer good at his job? Of course, but more importantly he has that sandy hair and a beard so unkempt that it feels as though he's doing it on purpose. Pure, unadulterated Jurgen – the addition of glasses to the mix was a nice extra flourish, too.

Kornmayer isn't the only one, though. Lucas Leiva, the former Liverpool player, got himself a pair of Klopp-style glasses back in 2016. He didn't look remotely like his former manager before, or indeed since, but for those few months the resemblance was uncanny. Coincidence? I think not.

Maybe it goes even deeper than this. It could be that

Klopp sees the look in his players' eyes when he doles out hug after hug and wishes he could know what it feels like to get that kind of embrace. Until technology reaches the stage where he can clone himself, the only solution is to develop an army of Kloppelgangers.

There's a reason why people talk about 'strength in numbers'. However powerful you are on your own, that power is multiplied by those fighting your corner. Of course, I'm not suggesting that you track down others in the world who look like you (that might start getting creepy really quickly). But while you and your mates don't *need* matching outfits or similar looks, it obviously can't hurt. After all, it didn't do the Power Rangers any harm, and if you didn't grow up wanting to be like the Power Rangers then you're lying.

HUG IT OUT

Jurgen is clearly a caring, loving man and, as I've already lightly touched on, you can see that with the embrace he wraps around each and every one of his Liverpool players, to the point that you can sense the 'no, don't let go' in their eyes. He makes people feel loved and wanted, but within that caring approach there occasionally also needs to be space for him to look after number one.

If you're still not convinced of the power of a Klopp hug, have a word with Jim Allgren, the American radio producer who dressed up as Klopp and travelled more than four hours just to get an embrace from Jurgen at a press conference in July 2019. 'I wasn't looking for anything more than a chance to get one of those hugs and tell the boss how much we appreciated him, and to have a laugh over it with friends,' Allgren told the *Liverpool Echo* at the time. And all he had to do was ask, 'What about a hug, boss?' I've heard stories of people accidentally calling their boss 'dad', but this was that flipped. Who can blame him? We all, regardless of the team we support, see Jurgen Klopp as football's collective father.

Oh, and what did Klopp himself say upon seeing Allgren, complete with that ever-so-familiar hair and beard combo? 'You look like my f**king doppel-ganger!' There was no way he was going to blank a man who was essentially yet another version of himself. If you love yourself, you love yourself in all forms.

Maybe you've never been a big hugger, and maybe Jurgen Klopp has changed that about you. I definitely used to be in that school of thought. If you're still a bit hesitant, there's no harm in giving it a go – by bringing friends and family physically closer, you're showing how close you are in spirit at the same time. If you're reading this and thinking you're 'not a hugger', bear in mind everyone is not a hugger right up until the moment they are one, and I don't know any people who have demoted themselves back to non-hugger after making the switch. I bet there's someone out there reading this who has found themselves hugging family, friends or both a great deal more in recent years without being able to pinpoint exactly when it started. I'd wager it's some point after October 2015, and I could make a good guess about what – or who – inspired it.

Q: You've forgotten your friend's birthday is tomorrow and you haven't got time to buy a card or present – WWJKD?

A: Surely your presence at the birthday party is the only gift your friend needs. Well, it would be if you hadn't used that same line last year. It's time for some decisive action and that means channelling your inner Klopp. Turn up to their house two hours before the party starts, greet them with a big hug and tell them to get in the car – you've got a surprise in store. By calling in some old favours, in the space of just a few hours you've set up a scavenger hunt. Overelaborate? Yes. Absolutely necessary? Also, yes. While your friend's out collecting clues, make your way to the party venue via a stop at the off-licence for a bottle of champagne. That part of the gift is purely symbolic – the journey is the real prize.

PICKING SIDES

It might take a bit of imagination, but I want you to picture Klopp as a child in the school playground. It's going to be tricky, I know. When someone has such childlike wonder as a grown adult and father, how can you figure out what he was like growing up? The clues are there, though.

Young Jurgen knows what it's like in both worlds. He's the athlete and the kid with glasses. He's smart enough to know that his self-worth isn't tied to his footballing ability. And he knows picking teams in playground games of football isn't just about selecting the best players.

The other playground captain – let's call him Jens, with apologies to any real-life Jenses out there – loads his team with the sporty kids. The bigger boys who act as natural bullies. They laugh among themselves as young Jurgen goes another way. His first pick is the quiet kid who stays behind after class for extra credit. Next, he grabs the captain of the chess team. Then the kid who everyone thinks has always been a bit weird. There's no real explanation, but every class has a weird kid, right? The laughs get louder, but then the game starts.

Klopp might only be 11 years old, his voice yet to break and his laugh yet to get anywhere close to booming, but he has another power: people listen to him. The bigger boys have strength and skills, but Team Klopp is giving its all. After one of the bullies gets nutmegged, his team-mates turn on him and start laughing in his face. When the weird kid scores a goal, the other captain starts a fight with his goalkeeper. Klopp's team win the 15-a-side game by one goal, and they all embrace when the bell goes to call them back in for class.

When you were growing up, it was a lot easier to choose your friends. You weren't old enough to cave in to peer pressure about who was 'cool' and you weren't choosing your mates based on superficial things. Jurgen Klopp has brought back that idea of giving everyone a chance, no matter how goofy they look or how eccentric they appear. It's worked OK for him, so it can definitely work for you too. Next time you're in a position to choose who you want to spend your time with, take a Klopp approach and think about who you'd have the most fun with.

'I take with me a bag full of the most positive memories and I hope you are too'

JURGEN KLOPP AT THE BORUSSIA
DORTMUND FAREWELL PRESS
CONFERENCE, MAY 2015[2]

Q: Your best friend comes to you in tears. He's been dumped by his partner of six years and you can see he's understandably distraught – WWJKD?

A: This calls for a hug, of course, but not just any normal hug. It's time for one of those transcendental, Klopp-style ones. The kind where you both hold on too long and let go too soon, but in a good way. You tell him it's OK to cry sometimes and then you reassure him with a well-timed 'we go again'. I said 'well-timed'. Unlike, well, you know where this is headed . . .*

---

* I'm sorry, Stevie G. You know I love you really.

GETTING THE GANG BACK TOGETHER

Every few years, we'll see a variation on this distinct subgenre of film: a group of friends come together to spend time in each other's company for the first time in a while, usually for the purpose of one last heist/night out/rekindling of youth [delete as applicable]. The setting will change, from America to a different part of America to, well, England (but one of the individuals will have spent some time in America in the intervening period). The details will switch up depending on the age and occupation of the people in question, but one thing always stays the same – the types of character involved.

There's the shy friend who has quietly succeeded in life by playing it safe. The wildcard, who gives the impression early on that he can't be trusted and then – guess what – demonstrates why he can't be trusted. And then there is the leader. The alpha. Or, in other words, the Jurgen Klopp type.

The qualities of the Klopp type can't be taught. He's shown you can still 'become' a leader while remaining approachable, even if that sounds contradictory. An aura is an aura because it goes beyond any kind of by-numbers. Think back to Bradley Cooper's character in *The Hangover* and Leonardo from *Teenage Mutant Ninja Turtles* (don't worry, I'm not going to judge you if you were more of a Raphael person). You can't quantify exactly why you'd want them to be your friend, or why you're drawn to trust them even when their behaviour doesn't warrant it. There's just that *je ne sais quoi*. The approachability blended with superiority, plus that mystery ingredient you can't put your finger on. They even get some of the best lines, which on top of everything else just seems unfair.

The thing is, even if you're different now, this person was once like you. Yes, even Jurgen Klopp once had idols. By becoming the sort of person who he might choose as his mate, you're becoming someone who others will want on their side too.

'I would say he's a friend. He's a fantastic person . . . I told him that the door is always open for him after his three years and [if] I'm still here, of course, then we will find a place for him'

JURGEN KLOPP ON LUCAS LEIVA
WHEN THE MIDFIELDER LEFT
LIVERPOOL FOR LAZIO[3]

3. **MENTALITY MONSTERS**

⚽ ⚽ ⚽

JURGEN KLOPP AND WORK

Chances are, you will remember your first boss. It doesn't matter if you have to cast your mind back decades or just a few weeks, you probably still have a pretty vivid memory of them. It doesn't matter if they taught you valuable life lessons or left you feeling dumber than when you started the job – the first boss always leaves an impression like nobody else.

Some of us start out with a 'down with the kids' sort of boss. The kind of person who adds you on Facebook and on a Friday afternoon takes the entire team out to the pub. They emailed you a meme exactly once, and it was one that was really, really, really popular in 2008.

It was the first time you'd seen it in years and it felt like you'd travelled through time or fallen asleep and woken up in a country that no longer existed. It was strange, sure, but it also showed that deep down they genuinely cared about what we thought of them.

Some of us, however, were stuck with a hard task-master straight off the bat. The kind who would leave the office at 3.30pm but somehow always knew if you were out of your seat a second before nine in the evening. You lost a ton of weight in that job because they made you feel guilty for going out for lunch or snacking at your desk, but it was character-building because it helped you form long-lasting relationships with your co-workers as the only other people who truly understood your suffering.

The best bosses, though, are those who leave such a great impression that you want to follow them wherever they go. They'll set up their own, brand-new company and get you to join by making you feel like you're the most important person in the world. But it's when they keep making you feel like that, long after you've joined, that you know your instincts were right.

You're going to be the boss of something at some point in your life, even if it's not in the most literal sense. For some of us, 'being a boss' means running a

300-employee company, while for others it's volunteering to coach your six-year-old's school football team. Your responsibilities might be different between one and the other, but in both cases you'll need to identify a leadership style. And there's nowhere better to start than by following Jurgen Klopp's lead.

BEING A GREAT BOSS

For a lot of Jurgen Klopp's Liverpool squad, Jurgen Klopp wasn't the first larger-than-life manager to lead them into battle. And he wasn't the first who might be described, in the words of David Brent, as a 'friend first, boss second, probably an entertainer third'. However, what is unique about him is the way he shows us the persona is not a gimmick. This is part of what makes him such a rounded person and such a great coach, rather than something he accentuates to hide his flaws.

'After the 2013 Champions League final at Wembley, which Klopp's Dortmund lost 2–1 to Bayern Munich, Klopp told the media that, "The only thing I can say is [that] it was great . . . only the result was shit",' Huw Davies recalls.

He tells me that, 'Although it's easy to assume it

was him [Klopp] being typically kooky, he said it with a straight face and clearly meant it. He swears more than most managers, but he wasn't doing this for a soundbite – he was just being honest. I still remember it for being a fun but also bittersweet, even touching moment.'

When I see moments like this, I don't view them as being manufactured to fit the *idea* of Klopp. He's doing this because he believes in it, and this is the kind of honesty that makes his players play for him from the first whistle to the last.

Klopp described his Liverpool players as 'mentality monsters' for the way they always fight to the end, and they wouldn't do this without a boss they *want* to fight for. Klopp has shown that if you want the same, you can achieve it with honesty and by showing your true self, not by hiding behind management-speak.

'I don't just want to win;
I also want to feel!'

JURGEN KLOPP[1]

THE FIVE TYPES OF FOOTBALL MANAGER

THE MIKE BASSETT

Mike Bassett: England Manager – one of the greatest-ever sports movies, which deserved Oscars, Baftas and every other award going[*] – was the best-ever depiction of a certain type of manager. A no-nonsense type of boss, straight out of the 1970s, when men were men and cigarettes were about 10 per cent of your average footballer's diet. Likely to rule that, if you're not in obvious physical distress at the end of a training session, you simply don't 'want it' enough. This all works surprisingly well, even in 2020.

---

[*] No, I have not rewatched it since the early 2000s, for the simple reason I do not want my perfect memories to be soured.

THE PHILOSOPHER

Spends press conferences speaking in meta-phors and spends training sessions stand-ing silently, presumably trying to come up with a new metaphor to use in his next press conference. Stints as a guest pundit during a World Cup or European Championship and draws confused looks from the regulars.

THE FOLLOWER

Once worked under a more senior, more famous manager. It was probably either a Mike Bassett or a Philosopher, and they clearly left a mark on the Follower. So much so that their name is invoked at least once a day, usually once an hour and – during team talks – once per sentence.

THE SCIENTIST

Prefers diagrams and PowerPoint presentations to human interaction. Come to think of it, you can't remember a single time he has spoken to you instead of just pointing at a board and drawing some demonstrative lines.

THE MAVERICK

Less dry than the Scientist but less basic than the Mike Bassett. This is often the kind of manager who forms the basis for the Follower's philosophy. This is the manager who knows how to interact with the media *and* with his players, and you can rely on him for a great soundbite on a regular basis.

For years, rival fans would mock Brendan Rodgers for his Brent-ism, especially when it came to the infamous *Being: Liverpool* documentary. In the fly-on-the-wall show, Rodgers presented his squad with three envelopes, each of which supposedly contained the name of a player who would let the team down that season. Of course, as we now know, the envelopes were empty.

Rodgers would probably have you believe it's a lesson in recognising that your talent and application were inside you all along. I'll argue it's a lesson in never trusting a man who presents you with an envelope. Tax bills, court summonses and requests to pick a meal for friends' weddings a year in advance have all proven me right in this regard. The envelope is just a glorified version of the meeting that should have been an email.

Jurgen Klopp, by contrast, is a friend, boss and entertainer all at once. He'll land you with a party that should have been a meeting; what ought to have been a chain email ends up, somehow, as a karaoke session. You're not sure how it works, but it does.

He still has an element of the 'How do you do, fellow kids?' mentality about him, though. It's just even this becomes an endearing quality. You know he's doing it for the right reasons. He was old before his time as a player, but there's still a little bit of youth to cling on to, and you'd be lying if you said there wasn't something admirable in the cheesiness. Make no mistake, though, it's still extremely cheesy.

Part of being a great boss isn't just reading from the same script as those under you; it's also making sure they won't kick up a fuss when they need to do the things they *don't* enjoy. If you believe every footballer in the world actually *enjoys* running more than 10 kilometres in every match, you've got another think coming. OK, yes, James Milner lives for this shit, but that's not the case with everyone. They'll do it, though, because when Jurgen Klopp asks them to do it they know there's a good reason why.

'I'm responsible for our bad performances, they are responsible for our good performances. That's quite an easy deal'

JURGEN KLOPP AFTER LIVERPOOL BEAT LEICESTER CITY IN 2016[2]

Q: Your three-man team has been nominated for an award, but there's only space for two of you to attend the ceremony – WWJKD?

A: Sure, your fantastic leadership is the main reason for the nomination, everyone knows that, but sometimes it's about more than that. You graciously tell the organisers you won't be attending yourself, but your two junior staff members will be taking the places. You've been to plenty of these before, after all, and who knows if they'll ever get another chance. The organisers immediately cave. You've called their bluff. You were the one they wanted there all along, so they give you an extra seat at the table.

BOSS, THA!

Could Jurgen Klopp's management style translate to a 'regular' office job? Absolutely. In fact, we already see elements of that in our day-to-day lives. The CEO who shows up to work in band t-shirts and tries to engage you in chats about pop culture? That's Klopp energy, put to poor use. The one who buys a ping-pong table for the office and organises a tournament involving the entire workforce? Pure Klopp. The CEO who introduces 'Beer Friday' and puts his card behind the bar at the local pub. You bet, my Klopp senses are tingling.

Just doing all of these things isn't enough to make someone a great boss, though. If it was, everyone would be doing it.

The problem with bosses like that is it's really easy to tell when they're trying too hard. It's also really easy to see through all the bluster as soon as it becomes clear this is all they have. Overcompensation becomes really funny when you've figured out that's what they're doing and they haven't figured out that you've figured it out.

Q: You show up for a job interview and get handed a baffling, ridiculously complex task the minute you walk through the door. You barely understand what it means, let alone how you'd go about tackling it – WWJKD?

A: First of all, make sure not to rush into things. There's a time limit on the task, but it's not unmanageable – use a minute to take stock of the situation rather than rushing straight into it. The primary objective is to make sure you don't rule yourself out of contention and, as soon as you've done that, you can go about showing them your qualities. Stay calm, complete the task as best you can and then wow them in the face-to-face part of the interview. Even if you weren't the best at everything, there's no way they'll be able to say no to your raw charisma and charm. And if you don't have raw charisma and charm, just throw in a couple of bad jokes. It's basically the same thing.

FOLLOW THE LEADER

The idea of Jurgen Klopp as an icon ought to be a tough sell. When you think about who young people look up to, it tends to be people their own age. People punching up and trying to make a better world for those who are like them. When you were a teenager, you didn't have a picture of a boss on your wall unless you were a massive Bruce Springsteen fan. The players are always supposed to be the stars, and the managers are merely the ones who facilitate that stardom. But somehow, something about Klopp has managed to cut through.

'Jurgen is also motivated by the people around him and by making people happy, so he understands just how much it would mean if Liverpool were to win the league,' Raphael Honigstein, who wrote one of the most important books about the manager, said in 2019. 'I think he would take either [the league or the Champions League] in a heartbeat, but it's not his choice to make, unfortunately.'[3] There has never been a sense of settling, though. Even after winning the Champions League in 2019, Liverpool kept pushing forward and breaking records. It wasn't the pinnacle – it was just the beginning. It took until January 2020 for Klopp to equal Pep Guardiola's record of the most Premier League Manager of the Month awards in one season – that's outrageous, however you look at it.

Therein lies the appeal of the man. Wanting to make people happy, above all else, is not something you can fake. Jurgen Klopp is the man in charge, sure, but there has always been a feeling that he's never elevated himself above those he is working for.

How much you like a boss tends to be in direct opposition to how much you notice them trying to make you like them, and indeed his flaws make him all that more endearing. If someone's robotic and efficient, you lose the human aspect.

Ask an outsider about Jurgen Klopp, and you'll get a few different responses. There is, of course, a minority who don't like the guy, but we'll skip past those folks for the time being. From the majority, you'll hear adjectives like 'relatable' or 'joyful', 'charismatic' or 'cheery'. These words have nothing to do with the tactical side of the game and, when people praise the abstract, motivational elements of a manager's character in this way, it can look like they're playing down how tactically complete he is on top of all that.

But just because he's a big personality doesn't mean that he's not a master tactician. 'I'd agree with those who say that his off-field persona distracts people from his tactical awareness,' Huw Davies says. 'Liverpool's fullbacks have just had a season in which they posted astonishing numbers, the likes of which we've never seen before – he didn't just tell them to work harder. In fact, even the idea that he's a motivator feels like it could be not just faint praise but false altogether.'

Grace Robertson, a football writer specialising in stats and tactics, has a similar outlook, telling me, 'In truth, I don't think any top manager today couldn't be described as a tactical thinker, and Klopp is no exception to this.' She adds, 'I had never personally pegged him as a pure motivator, but with his public persona this is obviously a sense he is more than happy to cultivate.'

So, Jurgen Klopp is a great tactician, something he sometimes doesn't get enough credit for, but, let's face it, so are all the other top coaches in his generation. Those are guys who end up being praised and respected as mentors but who are not *loved* in the same way. When you're asked to name your favourite video game, you don't give the honour to a driving simulator, however perfectly crafted it might be. You go for a *Mario Kart* or a *GoldenEye*, *because of* their flaws not in spite of them. You got into this world for excitement and surprises, not for everything to go exactly as anyone could predict it all the time. You go for the emotional pull as well as the technical qualities. You go for the occasional losses because they make the wins that much more powerful. You go for the system where you're taught to be better, but need to put in the hours yourself as well. You go for Jurgen Klopp.

Q: You're a year into a new job when your dream employer approaches you with an offer. You're not sure about it, though. As much as you'd love to work there, it feels just that little bit above your pay grade and they seem to have you confused with someone much more accomplished and experienced – WWJKD?

A: It's not like you to jump ship when you've got unfinished business. You're not going to abandon something good and leave others in an impossible position. You have faith in your own ability, and so should your dream employer. If they really care, and if you're really as good as they think you are, the opportunity will come along again. It doesn't matter if that's in a year's time, or two years, or ten. It'll be worth the wait.

'We don't save lives or things like that, we are not doctors. It's our job to let them [the fans] forget their problems for 90 minutes and then they can talk for three days about the last game and talk for two days about the next game'

JURGEN KLOPP, FROM LFCTV INTERVIEW, 2015[4]

4. FOR THE LOVE OF THE GAME

⚽ ⚽ ⚽

PLAYING WITH JURGEN KLOPP

If you're heavily into football, it's hard not to get super-competitive about, well, more or less everything. But what Klopp manages so well is his ability to temper his competitive streak (just look at the release in one of his sideline fist pumps) so that he can enjoy the play, focus on the end results and, ultimately, soak up the inevitable wins.

If you're one of the lucky ones, you support a team that wins more often than it loses, and, who am I kidding, it's easier to be competitive when you've got experience of winning. Getting massively fired up and overconfident about a bunch of losers? That's just not quite as fun, is it? But despite the losses, Klopp continues to come back to play – it's an admirable attitude to life and one we could all take on board.

When I spoke to Dan Austin, writer and editor for Liverpool.com, he told me: 'I'm fortunate enough to be able to stand on the Kop for every Liverpool home game, and make it to plenty of aways too. I could not count the amount of times I've stood in a ground and laughed my head off watching Klopp's Liverpool. There are honestly tens of times I've watched his team do something incredible and just instinctively burst out laughing, whether it be a stunning result that seemed impossible, a bombastic counterattack full of speed that puts a group of defenders on the floor, or him screaming at the Anfield main stand to clap louder whenever Adam Lallana wins a tackle. Klopp simply makes football the most joyously fun thing in the world.'

That level of joy would be powerful for any set of fans, but Jurgen Klopp's impact in recent years has been so meaningful in part because of how long the supporters of his two recent teams had been waiting for success. Borussia Dortmund had gone nearly a decade without a title when he ended the streak in 2011, surviving a brush with bankruptcy in the intervening period. And, as for Liverpool, everyone who went to school in England in the 1990s will have had a weird impression of Liverpool as this massive club, but one whose fame and size were alien to them since all the club's league titles were won before they knew what football was. But since the arrival of Jurgen Klopp, well, you know the story: the 2019 Champions League final was the big breakthrough victory, while a 97-point haul in the Premier League that same season would have been enough for a title in almost any other season – and a runaway success at that. And that's before you even start to look at the 2019–20 season, and the milestone of a full 12 months without a league defeat.

The key thing to remember, though, is that when Klopp joined both these teams, they were 'good' but they weren't ticking that big red box marked 'trophies'. As with all things in the game of life, Klopp had two choices: keep pushing until something clicks or walk away. He's showed all of us that the former path is the one worth taking.

Q: You've got the chance to win £10,000 on a TV game show, and all you need to do is choose a song for karaoke and get every single word right – WWJKD?

A: The smart move would be to pick a song with only a few words. 'Tequila' by The Champs, for example. Or even a fully instrumental song, leaving you free to just milk it on stage and walk away with the cash prize. You know that's not in the spirit of the game, though. You don't just want to win, you want to do it in style. You opt for 'Thunder Road' by Bruce Springsteen and you absolutely nail it, even 'singing' along to the instrumentals. By the end, you have the audience eating out of the palm of your hand.

ROLLING THE DICE

For most of us, playing professional football is an unlikely dream, one that just isn't going to happen. However, there is a different type of game that we all play – board games.

If we're going to discuss board games, we might as well cut to the most contentious and anger-inducing game of them all: Monopoly. Now, your first instinct might be that this is one of those games where thinking, 'What would Jurgen Klopp do?' won't serve you all that well. It's a game of ruthlessness, after all, and you win by grinding your opponents to dust and walking away having appropriated everything they own. Well, owned.

It feels distinctly un-Klopp by its very nature, but the main lesson here that you need to remember is that there's always more than one way to come out on top.

If a game was always about resources and nothing else, the same people would win every time. Borussia Dortmund would have got nowhere near Bayern Munich, and Liverpool getting the better of Manchester City would have been a pipe dream.

You need to make the right moves, but you also need a bit of luck. You need to bob and weave to land on Free Parking rather than Vine Street, or to hit Super Tax and gladly fork out £100 rather than parting with more than 10 times as much by going one either side and staying at your rival's Park Lane or Mayfair hotel.

It's the same in football. If you begin at a disadvantage, you need to make the best of your good moments and also secure a let-off when things aren't going so well. You need to hit five or six when you're on top and squeeze out a draw when you're up against it. It's a play Jurgen Klopp has near-mastered.

Now, there is one final Klopp tactic that I reckon would be a key part of his Monopoly strategy and that's his unrelenting charm and charisma. Of course, I have no hard evidence that being likeable has a direct influence on your chances of creating a Monopoly oligarchy, but, let's face it, if you were playing against Jurgen Klopp then you wouldn't begrudge him the odd slightly generous trade and you certainly wouldn't take pride in bankrupting him. This alone might be enough to will his car (he's always the car because he knows you want to play as the dog) around the board while avoiding any devastating punishment. Soon enough, the playing field is levelled and the momentum is with him. Boom.

'I sometimes try to imagine how it is in all the living rooms all over the world'

JURGEN KLOPP[1]

A DIFFERENT BALL GAME

The concept of team building is a bizarre one and something most of us will unfortunately have to endure at some point in our lives. If you haven't had the pleasure of it yet, it usually involves being stuck with people you can't stand for a morning (or day, if you're especially unlucky), and spending the whole affair trying to gravitate towards people you vaguely get along with already.

Jurgen Klopp, however, undoubtedly recognises the importance of true team building to powerful play on the pitch, and I think we can all comfortably imagine what it's like at a Liverpool team bonding session.

Picture the scene: it's a week into pre-season training. The players are building back up to full fitness, but not expected to be there just yet. The boss sees they need to reconnect as a group and introduces them to Fran, an expert in 'personal connection relations', whatever that means. Their day of activities begins with an arts and crafts course where they have to work together to design a new Liverpool shirt, followed by an afternoon of bowling. At least it beats double training sessions.

Sure, you've got your little cliques, but everyone – and I mean *everyone* – is rushing to be on the boss's team. It's basically the direct opposite of a *regular* work awayday, but then Jurgen Klopp isn't exactly a regular boss.

When I chatted to Steven Chicken about his thoughts on Klopp's management style, he said: 'It's always hard to say from the outside but it does seem like he has a much better understanding of the motivations of elite-level footballers than most other managers. I know it's easy when you're winning but you very rarely, if ever, hear of murmurings of discontent from the dressing room as you do at practically every other club – other than the sour grapes of a few players who haven't been playing because they just weren't good enough.'

Plus, this balancing act of being the boss while also being likeable is one that is very clear. As Steven went on to say, 'Modern players seem to need much more of an arm around them but also can't be allowed to stray into being spoilt and cosseted – they still need the occasional boot up the arse. That's a real tightrope but Klopp seems to walk it expertly. And he has to . . . the style of play demands it.'

Every manager will try to impose their own style on a new team, whether that means banning fast food, stopping players spending entire evenings on the Play-Station before big games, or even something as flat-out punishing as extra training sessions on Christmas Day. It's not a question of whether doing these things is necessary, but whether the players can be convinced that they're necessary. For that, you need to follow Jurgen Klopp's lead and not just earn trust, but make people *look forward to* these moments.

Q: You're at school during lunchtime and one of the bigger kids challenges you to a fight – WWJKD?

A: You know how the rules of the playground work. Backing out altogether isn't an option, even if you've never been the fighting type. Klopp once said he loves football because 'You can win against better teams if you work better together than them', and that's just another way of saying anything is possible with the right preparation. You agree to the fight, but only if you're allowed to set the time and place. The bully agrees, and you drag them to a boggy, mud-soaked football pitch on the rainiest day of the year. Oh, and you set it up for right in the middle of an actual game. A game that the other kid is supposed to be playing in. These conditions don't favour you, but the real test was showing up at all. You've fulfilled your part of the bargain, and anything they do from here on out will come back to bite them. Is it a win? Sure, why not, let's call it that.

HOW TO PLAY FIVE-A-SIDE
LIKE JURGEN KLOPP

In nearly 20 years of management, Jurgen Klopp has taught us a few things, but he's also needed to learn a little bit. Over that amount of time, though, you're able to refine your style and settle on something that works. Something that allows you to look at the game of football and make it work for you rather than the other way around. Here's how to do it like Klopp:

1. Find yourself a trademark move

Kerlon had the seal dribble. Muhammad Ali had the shuffle. Kareem Abdul-Jabbar had the skyhook. Others might be able to replicate your trademark once in a while, but it will belong to you. For Jurgen Klopp, this is the gegenpress. He wasn't the first to introduce this dynamic tactic to football, and plenty of others followed him in making use of it, but it's unmistakably a Klopp thing.

2. Know how to work the (sitting) room

The best managers in English football have always needed to find ways to get on the media's good side. Those who failed to do this from the get-go, like Graham Taylor in his England days and Andre Villas-Boas at Chelsea, didn't last all that long. Having a sense of charm isn't enough, though. You need to know when to turn it on and when to dial it down. Brian Clough was phenomenal at turning arrogance into an endearing quality, while Jose Mourinho became one of the best because he presented himself as one of the best (i.e. a 'Special One' and it became a self-fulfilling prophecy. Jurgen

Klopp didn't need his Liverpool team to be a roaring success on the pitch right away – he worked on winning people over on camera, and the longer people focused on that, the more time it bought him to get everything else right. And, boy, did he get it right.

When you're leading your five-a-side squad into battle, you do so knowing the worst thing that can happen is no one taking you seriously. Your fives team isn't just a bit of idle fun – well, at least if you want to win it isn't. The next time you've gone back to your mate's house to catch the end of whatever Champions League game is on after your Tuesday night game, it's worth remembering this. There's always time for a debrief, and if you've come from the Klopp school of management, you'll have them eating out of the palm of your hand and forgetting how preposterous the whole thing would look to anyone on the outside.

3. Get your soundbites in order

Is a wordless laugh a soundbite? For Jurgen Klopp, it is. The depth and sheer volume of his voice gives him a distinct, endearing quality that never seems to deviate. It's both punctuation and a catchphrase at once, and it just helps bring a warmth that you can't always deliver in a second language. This is probably why, however much you've tried to practise your laugh in the bathroom mirror, doing all you can to make it seem 'natural', it has always been impossible. The same goes for Klopp's trademark 'Boom', which is basic-ally the other side of the same coin.

In a world where football can seem a bit too, well, *serious*, injecting some normality into it is crucial. Even if you're putting every-one through their paces and convincing them to run their socks off, the least you can do is offer a smile and a laugh. And, yes, this

goes for five-a-side just as much as the professional game. More so, if anything, seeing
as you're all paying to play.

4. Get in the thick of the action

There's a wonderful clip on Liverpool's You-
Tube channel which sees Jurgen Klopp inter-
viewed by a child named Isaac and taught
some Scouse phrases. Countless players and
managers do media spots to help advance
their image, but unlike some others* he feels
like a natural. You wouldn't even be that surprised to learn he had some involvement in
the planning process, hand-picking an inter-
viewer who is the perfect level of relatable
– just like Klopp himself. When Jurgen Klopp
gets involved in something, to misquote
Homer Simpson, he uses his whole ass. He's

---

* Not naming names, but google 'Manchester
United Casillero del Diablo advert'. OK, I am
naming names.

a natural, and before the end of the interview he's talking like a born and bred Liverpudlian. While others might hesitate to do something like this, Klopp's willingness to take part helps explain why he's gone so far in football. If you show everyone else how committed you are, they'll be more inclined to follow your lead without complaining one bit. No one likes a five-a-side captain who doles out instructions and moans when they're not followed, only to then fail to heed his own advice. Klopp isn't just trying to let you know he's fighting for the team – more importantly, he's fighting from a position of equality.

'I'm aware of a lot of problems we have . . . and like every person with half a brain, I'm interested in solving them. But I really think we have to solve them *together*'

JURGEN KLOPP[2]

5. I LIKE IT LOUD

⚽ ⚽ ⚽

JURGEN KLOPP AND MUSIC

You might care too much about what other people think – I know it's something I've been guilty of at points in my life. I mean, for starters I began supporting a football team aged eight because I thought it would impress the cool older kids, and I'm stuck with them 25 years later. It's not even one of the *actually* cool teams, either, so I really lost out there.

That's not the only example, though. For more than 30 years on this earth, I've pretended to like certain bands, films and TV shows in an effort to impress other people. However, by embracing Jurgen Klopp's attitude to music you'll find a whole new way to enjoy life. If you've already reached this point, you're probably embracing it (feel free to skip ahead to the next chapter, although you'll miss Klopp of the Pops, which would be a shame). If not? Well, it's something to look forward to. Trust me. Not just because it'll impress me. Not even because it will impress Jurgen (although it absolutely would).

EMBRACING YOUR TASTE

There's something incredibly personal about listening to music. It's no surprise, then, that at some point in all our lives we care a lot about what others think about our music taste. Whether this led to spending hours watching *Top of the Pops* or *The Chart Show* and writing down (pen and paper, of course – this was long before iPhone notes) the songs you liked so you could burn them onto a CD, or frantically hiding that ska-punk album of *Grease* covers when your first girlfriend came over, we've all been there.

But one of the greatest life lessons Jurgen Klopp has taught us has nothing to do with football (haven't I already shown you that he's so much more than just a football manager?) – it's all about his attitude to music. For Klopp, his enjoyment is all that matters; he's all about just listening to the songs that make him happy.

It could be that you've never had a problem with embracing the music you like. You might be one of those people who never really let go of the pop music you listened to as a kid. The other lads in your football team might have given you some stick when you forgot to plug in your headphones and the Spice Girls started blaring out at full volume, but you were only really embarrassed by their reaction – you knew the music itself wasn't something to be ashamed of.

Perhaps you've got really into Christmas music? So heavily, in fact, that you play it in the car at all times of year. Your kids found it funny at first, almost endearing, but after the hundredth play of 'Stop the Cavalry', their enthusiasm is obviously waning.

But you don't care (too much) and this is true Klopp. The manager clearly doesn't let anybody else's opinions bother him. As he announced in 2013, he's a heavy metal man and I bet you can picture him rocking out in his car à la *Wayne's World*.

'I have never met a manager in football who was so naturally funny'

MARIO GOTZE[1]

> **Q: You've landed an audition on a reality TV show, but the person on before you has sung the song you had in mind – WWJKD?**
>
> **A:** Start singing the opening couple of bars of the song in question, and then, just as you notice Simon Cowell preparing to intervene, you hit him with a curveball, not just switching genre but switching the song altogether. Who knew 'All I Want for Christmas Is You' could flow into 'Welcome to the Black Parade' so seamlessly? Was this your plan all along? Only you know the answer.

A HEAVY METAL LIFE

For Klopp, heavy metal shapes his football as well as his life. He first used the phrase when his Borussia Dortmund team went up against Arsene Wenger's Arsenal and it was clear that this genre suited his persona perfectly. He said, 'I think he likes having the ball, playing football, passes . . . it's like an orchestra. But it's a silent song, yeah? I like heavy metal.'[2]

What does this mean? How *can* we know when what *it* is is open to interpretation? In some ways, heavy metal football has outgrown the man who coined the phrase and become whatever you want it to be. In others, though, it could not exist without Jurgen Klopp. And Jurgen Klopp, as we know him, could not exist without it.

It's a sporting mentality but also a personal one. You're the lead performer, belting out banger after banger on stage against a backdrop of crashing guitars and regrettable eighties haircuts, but you're also the drummer keeping the beat to make sure the singer can thrive. Klopp's football carries this quality. It's clear to see who the frontman is, or who the frontmen are, with Sadio Mane, Mo Salah and Roberto Firmino taking turns to assume the role of Liverpool's David Lee Roth.

The fullbacks are the guitarists, starting out on the sidelines but muscling in with a devastating solo when you least expect it. You still need the metronome, though. The person (or people) without whom the stars couldn't exist. If James Milner was in your heavy metal band, he'd be on the drums. Or maybe the triangle. But Klopp would let him know he was the most important element, even when that wasn't strictly true.

Q: You're the best man at a wedding and the band has cancelled with a day to spare – WWJKD?

A: Get someone to courier instruments, amps and all the rest to the wedding venue, and break off from your speech to launch into an impromptu rendition of 'Welcome to the Jungle'. You don't just stop there, though – you've got a whole three-hour set to work through. It doesn't even matter that you're horribly out of tune.

Maybe you like your football to be more like classical music, with big orchestral numbers. Sure, the crescendo of a beautifully crafted goal can be pleasing, but that's assuming the hours of build-up haven't put you to sleep before you even reach that point.

Perhaps pop music is more your speed. Bouncy, flighty tunes that play to the masses. I hear you – there's a reason the genre has always had an audience – but it's all too predictable. Everyone else on the pitch knows what's coming; they've seen all these goals before. Heavy metal football, though? That grabs you in ways you didn't expect, hitting you with something you really weren't ready for. It doesn't matter if it isn't the cleanest – by the time anyone is in a position to offer a critique, two, three, four goals have already flown past the opposing goalkeeper.

'I had heard of [Jurgen Klopp] for a couple of years already, but he really hit my radar when Dortmund started challenging in Europe. He seemed like the face of this new wave of fast, transition-based German sides that seemed set to take over football,' Grace Robertson recalls. In the same way, it has become easy to retro-fit the idea of heavy metal to Klopp's football – even if it's not something the manager described in those terms at the very start. It's easy to recognise it as something that has always existed, with or without that name.

It's the same reason Klopp has always been a coat-

and-tracksuit manager. He's happy to leave the suits and ties to the more orchestral types, because there's no way you can keep your collar starched and rid yourself of sweat patches under the arms of a white shirt when you're headbanging for 90 minutes.

It's reflected in those watching, too. Breakneck speed and pedal-to-the-metal guitar work have the same impact – people will get really, *really* into the moment. Do people enjoy other forms of football in the same way? I don't know, and frankly I don't want to know.

The volume and pace aren't restricted to the heavy metal football itself. The roar of the crowd grows in an effort to suck the ball into the goal. Sure, you might lose your voice, but the game will be over as a contest by then. Energy and intensity are the stars of the show, and you leave with your ears ringing, but in a good way.

For too long, we've been preached to about the value of playing football a certain way. What this risks is a sense that we need to live our lives this way too. Sure, sometimes you'll want to see a master of their craft intricately hit all the right notes in the right order, but you can be a great craftsman without that. After all, you're always more likely to have fun if the people you're watching are enjoying themselves just as much.

Now, I'm not saying you need to enjoy heavy metal to thrive, but there's no harm in giving it a go. In your head, it might be in that pile marked 'Uncool: Do Not Touch' along with show tunes and Eurovision, but you made that pile a long time ago. Things have changed, and you've opened yourself up to new experiences everywhere else in your life, so why not here too? Even if it's not for you, being open to new experiences is a sign of growth in and of itself. Jurgen Klopp got to where he is by listening to others while keeping his own individual streak, and that seems to have worked out pretty well.

'We are like a music band, with their own instrument. Jurgen is the band leader, and others are behind him playing the bass guitar or drum. I'm not sure which instrument is mine!'

LIVERPOOL COACH PETER KRAWIETZ, INTERVIEW WITH THE *DAILY TELEGRAPH*, JANUARY 2016[3]

BECOME THE LIFE OF THE PARTY

You don't get into heavy metal without being able to play an instrument (including vocals). It's just a case of playing in a way that's more fun and more immediate, and doing it right up until the point where you run out of energy. If you've ever been on a pub crawl in a European city, the metal bar you inevitably arrive at after five or six drinks is always the best one. There's a reason they don't take you there earlier in the night – well, two reasons. First off, metal bars gain an extra-special aura under cover of darkness, when it feels like you're going on an adventure. And secondly, if the night started there, no one would be able to convince you to leave. The 'pub crawl' would just be a one-stop party, descending further and further into chaos as the night progresses. Heavy metal energy makes for great parties – you can see that same infectiousness in Jurgen Klopp, and you can take that energy into your own parties too, even if there's a quick break for a pop power-hour around 2am.

You think Jurgen Klopp doesn't still have the guitar from the band he set up as a teenager? I'm willing to bet good money it's still there in his study at home, and it's not a case of keeping it in mint condition as a collectable. You can see when a guitar has been handled with love rather than with care. Every scratch and every dent has its own story. Maybe he smacked the neck against a wall when trying to serenade an old flame. Maybe he scratched it up really bad when rushing across town to play an impromptu set at a friend's birthday party. It's never 'just wear and tear', though.

Klopp isn't the guy who pulls out an acoustic guitar at a party; he's the guy who holds his *own* party as an excuse to get out the *electric* guitar. Sure, you don't *always* want to be that guy, but part of releasing your inner Klopp is knowing exactly when the time is right.

He's not the protective type, either – he'll let everyone have a go. He'll ease people in with some of the more mainstream bands of the era. Some Def Leppard here, a bit of Alice Cooper there – maybe he'll even stray into poppier territory like Bon Jovi. Within minutes, though, he'll have decided that's not quite heavy enough. Before you know it, it's Metallica time and you've knocked back a full can of beer* in about eight seconds.

---

* These situations don't call for wine, be it an expensive bottle of burgundy from Sir Alex Ferguson's private collection or a Mauricio Pochettino-approved Argentinian Malbec.

If you're thinking Jurgen Klopp doesn't strike you as the kind of person who will ever run out of energy, well, maybe you're right. If anyone could put together a three-hour heavy metal concept album, all delivered at breakneck speed, he's your man.

You can start planning that next house party now. There's nothing wrong with spending hours curating the perfect playlist, but it shouldn't be the be all and end all – sometimes the mood will call for something different, and sometimes it's worth taking a step back and letting someone else add their own choices to the Spotify queue. You'll always be safe in the knowledge that you've got some heavy metal bangers in reserve for later on – it's still *your* party at the end of the day.

JURGEN KLOPP'S TOP FIVE HEAVY METAL BANGERS

Now you know what heavy metal football means, you can probably figure out what it looks like on the pitch. This doesn't mean instruments strewn across the centre circle and defenders tripping over guitar cords as they try to intercept a cross. Instead, it's high-octane stuff with non-stop energy. Here are five games which show Klopp's heavy metal football at its purest:

1. Liverpool 3–0 Manchester City, 2017–18 Champions League

Champions League knockout games are proper epics, with their 180-minute run-time, and anyone who prefers explosive dive-bar gigs to fancy sit-down concerts will know 180 minutes is much, much too long for their tastes.

What do you do in this situation, then? You chop down the number of meaningful minutes and neck your beer at the side of the stage while everyone else is uncorking their bottle of wine in front of the orchestra.

Ninety minutes? Nope, still too long, even with an interval.

Thirty-one minutes? Now we're talking. That's how long it took Klopp's Liverpool to open up a decisive 3–0 lead and end City's Champions League run.

23: Number of goals scored by Jurgen Klopp's Liverpool in the 2017–18 Champions League group stage –the record for an English club.[4]

2. Liverpool 3–1 Manchester City, 2019–20 Premier League

If you think heavy metal is repetitive, you're mistaken. You might get variations on a theme, but while the sensation is the same the delivery is different.

Another 3–0 lead against Pep Guardiola's orchestral football? It might sound familiar, but Klopp's heavy metal footballers only waited half as long before cutting to the chorus.

1–0 after six minutes. 2–0 inside the first 15. By the time you've figured out whether the first couple of songs were really that good, the guitars of the next banger have already kicked in.

10 January 2020: The day Jurgen Klopp equalled Pep Guardiola's record of four Premier League Manager of the Month awards in the same season.[5]

3. Arsenal 1–2 Borussia Dortmund, 2013–14 Champions League (aka the game that started it all)

Wenger's Arsenal played beautifully, but as Klopp said a couple of weeks after the game, it was time for classical music to stand down and let metal take its chance.

Klopp came to London, home of Motörhead and Iron Maiden, and dismantled the orchestra when it was at its most settled. It took 17 seconds for an Arsenal attack to turn into a winning goal for Dortmund when striker Robert Lewandowski finished off a counterattack.

As Jurgen Klopp knows, the best heavy metal intros need to be short and sweet.

4. Borussia Dortmund 4–0 Freiburg, 2011–12 Bundesliga

Klopp's Dortmund lost three of their first six Bundesliga games in 2011–12, but I guess they were just tuning up.

The next 28 games brought 23 wins and five draws, and a *lot* of entertainment. Sometimes it was *too* exciting, like in the 4–4 draw with Stuttgart, but it mostly followed the same format. Blow teams out of the water, then keep at it just in case.

They'd already won the title by the time Freiburg arrived for the final game of the season. Time to ease off? Don't be silly.

We all know what happens when a heavy metal band tries out new softer material, and Klopp and his team weren't going to run that risk. Four goals arrived within 39 minutes of the first whistle – you know, just in case anyone was worried about false advertising.

28: Number of games Jurgen Klopp's Borussia Dortmund team went unbeaten on their way to winning the Bundesliga in 2011–12.[6]

5. Norwich City 4–5 Liverpool, 2015–16 Premier League

The great thing about heavy metal football – and heavy metal in general – is that even when it doesn't come off *exactly* as planned it's still lots of fun.

When Klopp took his team to Carrow Road in 2016, someone mixed up all the instruments seconds before kick-off and it made for the most chaotic football match in recent memory.

If the other team has scored three goals

from four shots, you've got to turn to plan B. And plan B in heavy metal terms is just to thrash wildly in the hope that something happens.

Liverpool got back from 3–1 down to 4–3 up. Then Norwich scored again in the 92nd minute. Then Liverpool won the game in the 95th. Then Klopp had his glasses knocked off his face in the celebrations.

It was like one of the Black Sabbath gigs that even Ozzy Osbourne doesn't remember playing. Pure mayhem.

BE TRUE TO YOUR ROOTS

We shouldn't be all that surprised by any of this, really. Klopp was born in Stuttgart, home of Porsche and Mercedes. Extreme speed and literal metal are in his blood.

Away from English-speaking countries, Germany has one of the healthiest metal traditions. Scorpions. Rammstein. Helloween. All varying levels of loud and fast, and all as German as they come. Head to any metal gig in Germany and you'll find tons of enthusiastic fans, giving it their all until they have no energy left.

Klopp grew up with the greats of heavy metal, too. Born in 1967, his formative years came when the genre dominated the mainstream with some massive crossover albums.

Who can't picture a 20-year-old Jurgen rocking out to Guns N' Roses' debut album *Appetite for Destruction*, or stunning his high-school friends in the Black Forest by introducing them to Iron Maiden's *The Number of the Beast*? Has he gone to a party in fancy dress as Gene Simmons from Kiss, doing a suspiciously efficient job with the make-up? Let's just say you can't rule it out.

When you bear this in mind, Liverpool doesn't just seem like the best city for him to manage in, but the only real option. Liverpudlians take pride not only in music, but in music *from Liverpool*. From The Beatles to The Coral, The La's to the Lightning Seeds, it's a city that celebrates its own.

'As soon as Klopp first spoke in his Melwood press conference, though, it was clear that he was a perfect match,' Dan Austin tells me. 'He spoke about football as something emotional, focused on collective responsibility, and emphasised his desire to give supporters something to enjoy and believe in outside of day-to-day life. All of that is in keeping with the mentality and belief system of Liverpool as a city. Scousers are people who pride themselves on solidarity, having a good time, and believing in a better future.

'The way Klopp spoke proved his personality and belief system were on the same wavelength as us, and I knew then that no matter what happened on the pitch, he would love Liverpool and Liverpool would love him.'

If you're from Liverpool yourself, you won't need reminding of any of this, and Jurgen Klopp has endeared himself to football fans by recognising the value of local identity as well as everything else. However, if you live elsewhere, perhaps it's time to ask yourself how attached you are to bands and singers with whom you share a hometown. There's nothing quite like seeing Mike Skinner in Birmingham, Stormzy in London or the Arctic Monkeys in Sheffield, and that counts double if you've had those shared experiences growing up.

'I started watching YouTube clips, press conferences, highlights of Dortmund performances and I'll admit I was immediately smitten,' says Hari Sethi, who became extremely aware of Klopp in 2014.

'I liked the rough-around-the-edges nature to him, the fact that he seemed to speak honestly, not with typical manager doublespeak and that his players/fans clearly adored him. As someone who was already a little cynical towards Rodgers as the '14–15 season unfolded, I convinced myself he would be an ideal fit for the city, let alone the club.'

There are some managerial marriages which have felt very 'wrong place, wrong time'. Brian Clough's 44 days at Leeds is the obvious example, while Roy Hodgson and Liverpool never really felt like a great fit. When things click, though, like they have with Jurgen Klopp, you wonder how the team and the man in charge ever survived before they were together.

TOP OF THE KLOPPS

There was a point in my life when I realised I was missing an element of tension and excitement. At first, I wondered whether it was just a side effect of getting older, but then I remembered another reason. After years glued to the radio listening to the Top 40 countdown, sometimes taping songs and making sure to press 'stop' before the DJ started talking over the final notes, that disappeared when music became something you listened to online without interruptions and discovered through algorithms. It's time to bring back the traditional countdown, and with this being a book about Jurgen Klopp, it needs a heavy metal flavour.

Stick this on at the gym when you're trying to get yourself pumped up for an intense session. Or in the car for your next long drive, when you need to properly rock out. Or perhaps you want to use it before the next team talk for the team you coach on the weekends. Unleash your inner Klopp, even if you didn't think you had it in you.

10. **Van Halen – 'Jump'**
    (up and head a free kick into the back of the net)
 9. **Iron Maiden – 'Run to the Hills'**
    (double sessions)
 8. **Guns N' Roses – 'Paradise City'**
    (Liverpool open-top bus parade remix)
 7. **Metallica – 'One'**
    (the only league position that matters)
 6. **Twisted Sister – 'We're Not Gonna Take It'**
    (to the corner)
 5. **Slayer – 'Raining Blood'**
    (red machine in full effect)

4. **Europe – 'The Final Countdown'**
   (this one's pretty self-explanatory)
3. **Bon Jovi – 'You Give Love a Bad Name'**
   (sorry, did I say 'Love', I meant 'Löw')
2. **Whitesnake – 'Here I Go Again'**
   (not on my own)
1. **Scorpions – 'Rock You Like a Hurricane'**
   (what? You thought we weren't going to put a German band on here?)

'My mother said it, my father said it: number one are The Beatles. I liked Genesis and I liked, long ago, Kiss. The lead singer had a very long tongue. He was crazy!'

JURGEN KLOPP, INTERVIEW WITH LIVERPOOL FC YOUTUBE, NOVEMBER 2015[7]

6. THE TASTE OF SUCCESS

⚽ ⚽ ⚽

FOOD AND DRINK WITH JURGEN KLOPP

Food and football have a strange relationship. There's a lovely nostalgia about meals which, in any other circumstances, would be considered 'bad'. Cheap pies filled with mystery meat. Hot dogs that are somehow too hot and too cold at the same time. Bovril.

Why should you settle for these sub-par snacks, though? Did Jurgen Klopp settle for Simon Mignolet, Alberto Moreno and Jordon Ibe? Of course not. All three played in his first Liverpool game, but now they're nowhere to be seen.

There's a difference between being a perfectionist

and just wanting better for yourself. Brendan Rodgers' time in charge of Liverpool, immediately before Klopp, was akin to an average burger with occasionally great sauces. But why be content with the luck of the draw when you can switch it up for prime beef that stands on its own?

There are two types of food connoisseur. You've got the pretentious type, who will put stock in famous restaurants and make a point of going somewhere because a celebrity included it on their Instagram story; and there are those who know exactly what they want and how it should be. Jurgen Klopp, quite clearly, is the second of these. He'll pick some of the less obvious menu items – a midfielder from relegated Newcastle here, a left-back from relegated Hull there – and turn them into a gourmet meal because they complement the other ingredients.

'I've been impressed by how he's managed to keep players who've had more peripheral roles at the club motivated and happy, though perhaps this can also be put down to the recruitment process and signing of players with a "team first ethic",' Hari Sethi tells me, while Dan Austin points to how the manager 'has converted players like Gini Wijnaldum and James Milner into footballers with a completely different position and playing style compared to their previous careers, and reinvigorated the careers of some who plenty thought had permanently been written off, like Dejan Lovren and Divock Origi'.

When you're cooking for a crowd, you're never likely to find yourself dealing with a group of people with identical tastes. Part of your task will come down to compromising on your own tastes to make everyone happy, but there's also skill involved in letting everyone feel included even when they don't get their first preference.

THE WURST OF BOTH WORLDS

Before Jurgen Klopp arrived on the scene, calling someone the barbecue chef of football might have felt like a coded insult. Not any more. Indeed, the thought of going to an *actual* barbie hosted by him feels just as appetising as watching him cook up that clunkiest of clichés, the 'feast of football'.

Hosting a barbecue for a dozen people requires perfect timing, making sure everything is cooked through but not burned and taking just as much care over the salads and vegan options as the main-event meats, all the while ensuring you can still handle your hosting duties. Some people need a series of alarms and handwritten notes for this – failing to prepare means preparing to fail, and all that – but enough practice makes everything that bit easier. If you take a leaf out of Jurgen Klopp's book, you'll soon be able to do it by feel alone. No one can teach instinct, but don't let that stop you working with the instincts you already have.

It's the middle of July, and it's the day you've been waiting for since the start of the year. That's right, it's Jurgen Klopp's annual summer barbecue.

The Klopp barbecue is like a Nando's black card or a trip in a private jet. You've heard stories about it, and it sounds glorious, but you refuse to believe them until you get the chance to see it for yourself.

People have told you about the spread on offer – oh, the spread. Bratwurst, bockwurst, leberkase, kasekrainer, currywurst (with homemade curry ketchup, of course) and knackwurst. There are stories of the Klopp family-recipe potato salad, too. Apparently, the secret ingredient is love.

But stop. You can't get too carried away. It's probably just part of Klopp's aura. He probably doesn't even do any of the grilling. Even if he does, there's no way it can be as good as you've built it up to be in your head, right? Right?

> **Q: You're hungry but you don't have much food in the house and it's snowing outside – WWJKD?**
>
> **A:** It's OK, you can improvise, just like Klopp did when he needed a left-back and all he had was James Milner and tens of hours of coaching time. Get some instant noodles, a couple of slices of burger cheese, a fried egg and the five pickled jalapeños you have resting at the bottom of a jar. Mix them all together and sprinkle some cornflakes on top for texture. Drizzle with hot sauce. Boom! A filling,* nutritious** meal.

---

* Citation needed.
** More than one citation needed.

MAKE SURE NO ONE GOES HUNGRY

You arrive at 12:00 sharp. You never normally turn up on time to things, but you think if you show up early doors then Klopp might shake your hand. Obviously, everyone else has had the same idea, but that doesn't stop him greeting you with a hug.

'Try one of these pretzels,' he says. 'I baked them myself.' Each one is bigger than your entire face.

When you showed up, you were expecting to see people drinking from two-pint steins, but it turns out you weren't thinking big enough. Yards of beer. Metres of beer for those who never 'got' the imperial measurement system. A replica of the Champions League trophy filled with beer. At least, you *hope* it's a replica. Surely he wouldn't . . . no, that's ridiculous.

You wash down your pretzel with a bottle of Pilsner. You could have chosen from a range of wheat beers, fruit beers, dark beers, wines, schnapps or soft drinks, though. You make a mental note to try those later on (but maybe not the soft drinks). Klopp laughs at your indecision and goes back to flipping burgers and turning sausages before moving them onto a tray to the side of the barbecue. He's wearing a novelty Bayern Munich apron which his son bought him as a prank. If you don't follow Klopp's lead and lean into the joke, then everyone ends up laughing at you instead of with you, and that's no fun. Lesson number one: when you're hosting people for a meal, always make sure they're well fed.

KLOPPTAILS:
COCKTAILS À LA JURGEN

Jurgen Klopp might be a beer drinker, but he's inventive enough to try his hand at the mixology game. No doubt these recipes would be enough to earn the Klopp seal of approval.

Mainz a Daiquiri: Fresh strawberries muddled with white rum and sugar, topped with strawberry purée and a dash of whipped cream to mimic the colours of the 1. FSV Mainz 05 kit. Drink upside-down for away games.

The Yellow Wall: Advocaat and lemonade, with a shot of peppermint schnapps to be dropped in after serving. In honour of Borussia Dortmund's iconic fanbase.

The Gegenpress: Jägermeister, condensed milk and espresso, downed in one while sprinting.

Borussia Teeth: Dark rum, caramel and chocolate syrups and yellow chartreuse, layered to mimic the black and yellow Dortmund home kit. Limit of two per person. Dentist visit recommended.

The Liver Bird: Tomato juice, vodka and a raw quail's egg. Season to taste.

The Front Three: Brazilian cachaça, Senegalese bissap and Egyptian tea, to honour Liverpool's front three of Roberto Firmino, Sadio Mane and Mohamed Salah. Shaken well and served long with ice. Non-alcoholic version also available.

'I'm not the best drinker
– I need two beers and
it's enough. Klopp's miles
better at drinking alcohol
than me!'

DAVID WAGNER
REFERENCE FOR P126 TK

SET A HIGH BAR

What's your favourite bar? I'm not talking your local, where you know everyone and the bartender has your order waiting for you when you walk through the door. I don't even mean your regular haunt where you go to watch the football, where you have your 'lucky' match-day rituals and can always let off some steam, win or lose.

No, I mean your *dream bar*. It's probably not in your hometown, or if it is then it's too expensive to visit regularly. It's more of a birthday or anniversary option, where you can make a special occasion really special. It's the sort of place where you'll try a fancy wine that costs as much for a glass as you'd normally pay for a bottle. They have the sort of whisky that's best enjoyed in a den filled with cigar smoke, and the kinds of cocktails best enjoyed in 1920s Paris.

Most importantly, though, it feels exclusive but also inclusive. The staff are welcoming but not sycophantic. The drinks are fancy but you genuinely like them rather than having to pretend to. In short, it's the kind of place you'll recommend to everyone looking for a memorable evening out.

Now, you might be wondering what this has to do with Jurgen Klopp. The answer is – everything.

The football played by Klopp's teams, when they're fully on song, is some of the best you've ever seen and some of the best you ever *will* see. It's full of technical quality and tactical brilliance – you can't get those kinds of results *without* these qualities. If a fine Bordeaux or an aged Scotch is good enough, you'll willingly listen to the sommelier explain the process. Even if you didn't think you cared to begin with, there's something captivating in someone breaking down brilliance and helping you understand a tiny bit more.

It can't just be about that, of course. Scientific breakdowns are interesting when they're *not* the norm, but after a while you're left thinking, 'This is fine, but so what?' Not naming any names, but you probably had a football team in mind when you were reading that sentence.

What you really need to do is partner this with a human side. Enter Klopp. He'll be enthusiastic about the drinks, but in a way that genuinely shines through. It's hard to buy the idea that someone really cares about something if the register in their voice stays constant, but when Jurgen Klopp really cares about something you can see his eyes light up and hear his speech quicken. It happens when he talks about his Liverpool players. It happens when he talks about music. It happens when he talks about his wife. I'd bet it even happens when he talks about the weather. If Jurgen Klopp cares about a drink and talks to you about it, then by the end of the night you'll care about that drink too. Now you've got a new contender for your favourite bar – the one where you've got a chance of running into Jurgen Klopp.

'We've had a beer and chatted about the game. It's quite refreshing because I don't get that feel with some managers in the Premier League, which is disappointing'

CHRIS WILDER, SHEFFIELD UNITED MANAGER, AFTER HIS TEAM PLAYED LIVERPOOL IN 2019[1]

Q: You're going for dinner at your in-laws' house and they've asked you to provide a dish. There's a lot of pressure on you to impress them – WWJKD?

A: This calls for a real showstopper. The sort of thing so good that they end up asking you for the recipe as you leave. You research meticulously, scrawling through old texts and social media posts to get a feel for what they normally like, then show up empty-handed and say, 'What? You don't think I'm enough of a dish myself?' They laugh hysterically. Then pause. You walk back out to the car and present them with a dish filled with the finest charcuterie you've been able to find *and* a homemade chocolate tart. You've also arrived with a selection of German beers, the kind you can't buy anywhere in the UK. If they're indifferent about the food, you can still share a drink with them.

IT'S ONLY A GAME

Let's return to the barbecue. By now everyone's pretty full – a two sausages per hour diet will do that to you by hour six, and that's before we get on to the rest of the food. Jurgen's created a new sandwich which you'll definitely be trying again. Two sausages, butter-flied and grilled, topped with pulled pork, a layer of potato salad, a dash of sauerkraut and some cheese melted on top with a blowtorch. A part of you regrets letting him use a blowtorch after his seventh beer, but sometimes you need to simply trust someone. And, anyway, that regret subsided as soon as you ran your hand under a cold tap and then took your first bite.

Klopp has dubbed the sandwich 'The Reuben Neves'. You ask him if he's dropping a hint about Liverpool's transfer policy and he just smiles. That might be the beer, though.

Things aren't winding down, far from it. You're just getting started. It's still supposed to be light out for another couple of hours, and someone has suggested drinking games. A few people are sitting on patio chairs, some are horizontal on the grass of the back garden, and the remainder are taking advantage of the fact that they can still stand up under their own power. That's the beauty of the Klopp experience. He cultivates an openness, an inclusivity, that leaves you desperate to find a way to spend more time in his company. When you're hosting friends for dinner or drinks, you don't want them looking at their watch and only staying as long as they feel it's polite to. If you're not forcibly removing someone from your hallway at 6am so you can get to bed, have you even had people round?

'Let's enjoy the world, let's enjoy the football, let's enjoy the journey and it's what we did so far – it was a good time'

JURGEN KLOPP[2]

7. GETTING YOUR VOTE

⚽ ⚽ ⚽

JURGEN KLOPP AND POLITICS

If the last few years have demonstrated anything, it's that a political background won't necessarily help you get far in actual politics. In fact, it might be a hindrance.

The public have spoken, and they've decided we need world leaders with diverse backgrounds. A congressman who used to be a punk musician.* A president who used to be a reality-show host. Whatever you'd describe Arnold Schwarzenegger as. And, inevitably, a *lot* of former sportsmen.

Ex-AC Milan striker George Weah was elected

---

* It's Beto O'Rourke, for those wondering.

president of Liberia in December 2017, winning 60 per cent of the vote, after trying and failing to run for office a decade earlier. Former world heavyweight champion boxer Vitali Klitschko entered parliament in 2012 and became mayor of Kiev two years later (at the third time of asking), admitting his political career was much tougher than his getting-punched-in-the-head career. One-time Liverpool striker Titi Camara spent two years as Guinea's sports minister and expressed pride at what he achieved in his short time in the role. Why can't Klopp be next?

There's only one thing to worry about when it comes to the prospect of Jurgen Klopp running for office – namely, that he'd be *too* successful. But that shouldn't stop you following his lead. Even if you've never considered yourself 'political', you might end up surprising yourself. Sure, you might not ever find yourself standing for public office, but that doesn't mean your life is free from politics. PTA meetings at your child's school. AGMs for your five-a-side team. Planning your works Christmas awayday. These are all political environments, whether you see them that way or not, and there's no better way to navigate them than by asking yourself what Jurgen Klopp would do in the same situation.

'I like that he's a socialist. Basically the only one in English football'

HUW DAVIES

WINNING THE POPULAR VOTE

If Klopp were to find himself forced out of football management – an unlikely scenario, I know – it wouldn't be hard to see him starting a new career in politics. He knows how to speak on camera. He knows how to use soundbites to push the narrative. He knows, perhaps more than anyone else in football, how to surround himself with a loyal group of people. In short, Jurgen Klopp is the epitome of a vote-winner.

That, in itself, feels like a rarity in football. There are plenty of players and managers who you'd relish seeing on the pitch but never even think of supporting at the ballot box. The reckless, heart-on-sleeve aggression of a great centre-back can be a hindrance as much as a help in real life. The subtlety and skill of an attacking midfielder will help unlock defences, but won't be loud enough to get through to floating voters. A goalkeeper can't be trusted as an all-rounder, or else he wouldn't be a goalkeeper.

There are plenty of topics that can divide groups of people who might otherwise sing from the same hymn sheet. Social issues. Economic issues. Things they didn't bother about five years ago but now care about more than anything else. And, yet, football remains the one element that can get these people together and allow them to put all of that to one side. Just think how many times you've joined in with a terrace chant out of pure instinct, without even really thinking about the words, just because you know the volume brought by thousands of voices speaking in unison can be more powerful than anything else.

In every office in the UK, it's becoming harder and harder to escape political divisions. It's something that affects everyone's day-to-day life, so this is only natural, but it can lead to rifts. I've even heard of some companies putting a blanket ban on 'politics chat' after it started distracting people from their actual jobs. Weird how the era of 'populist' politics has led to more divisions, isn't it? Taking a Jurgen Klopp approach can solve this problem, though, by figuring out what works for *everyone*. It's amazing how much easier it is to get people onside when something that benefits one group doesn't only do so at the expense of another. You don't even need to substitute out their political arguments and bring football arguments off the bench. Instead, we get that strange, unfamiliar thing called 'unity'. Remember that? I swear it's existed before.

'The best way to learn the job is if you have to do everything and nobody is really watching it'

JURGEN KLOPP[1]

Q: You're due to debate with a political rival live on TV but they don't show up. It's too late to reschedule, and the person chairing the debate is out of ideas – WWJKD?

A: Present your side of the argument anyway, just as planned. After all, you've spent days preparing for this moment and you're not going to let that work go to waste. Then, when it comes to your rival's turn, switch seats and pretend to be them. Complete with a fake nose and fake moustache – it doesn't even matter if they actually have a moustache. Spend the next 45 minutes darting from one seat to the other, donning and removing the disguise, and 'debating' with yourself. I'm not saying you have to put on a comedy accent when playing the part of the other person, but it certainly wouldn't hurt.

BUILD TRUST

The first media spots come next. Now, maybe you're one of those people who does things the proper way and reads the entire manifesto of all the major parties before coming to a decision, but you and I both know this isn't exactly common practice any more. If people can't do that for something as potentially life-changing as politics, they're hardly going to apply it to the everyday. That makes building trust essential in every aspect of your life.

It can take a while for a public figure to gain people's trust. Sometimes, if they miss their window, it might never happen. You've probably got an idea of who I'm referring to with that comment, and you're right. It's Unai Emery.

You don't get to choose what the public think of you, but you can give it a good go. The trick is making sure they think they've come to a decision all by themselves when you were the one pulling the strings all along.

'There was nobody I would have preferred to have as manager, and the fact that he came in and immediately felt like a perfect fit in terms of attitude, playing style and charisma only helped that impression,' Steven Chicken says.

'Don't forget that Liverpool's previous three appointments had been the ill-suited Roy Hodgson, a desperate plea for fan approval in Kenny Dalglish, and (though Rodgers did well at Liverpool) an appointment from mid-table Swansea City. Klopp was the first true superstar manager Liverpool had appointed since Rafael Benitez, and even then was a much larger-than-life figure than the quiet and considered Spaniard was when he arrived from Valencia.'

So, straight off the bat, a Jurgen Klopp political campaign doesn't need to *lead* with a detailed policy plan. That bit can come later. The first and most important thing for the public to know is they'll be voting for Jurgen Klopp. And for those of you keen to argue it's not a popularity contest, have you even looked at politics in the last 10 years?

Whether you're persuading your colleagues to get on board with your new project or convincing your children to study for their exams, earning trust is a crucial weapon in anyone's armoury. You don't have to be an elite football manager and you don't even need to have any political experience or ambitions. However, as is so often the case, Jurgen Klopp has a lesson you can follow at any turn.

JURGEN KLOPP'S
FIVE-POINT PLAN

A politician can't get elected on charisma alone. At least, not *just* yet. You need a manifesto of sorts. It's impossible to tell what it would look like if Jurgen Klopp was to run for election; but, on the other hand, it would be exactly – and I mean exactly – like this.

1. A nationwide ban on wind

The wind has caused Klopp problems before, not least in the 2019 Merseyside derby, but he's all about equality. He's not the type to control the weather for himself and leave others wanting. No wind for anyone, anywhere. There's no possible downside to this.

2. Change the national anthem to 'Wind of Change' by Scorpions

'God Save the Queen': dated; unoriginal lyrics; bland; reinforces divisions. 'Wind of Change': dynamic; from a golden era of music; timeless; brings people together. This one's a no-brainer, even without it syncing up with another key policy plan.

3. Free hugs for everyone

Obviously. Prime Minister Klopp will give out as many as he can, but you need to appreciate he's a busy man. There's a reason he's built his army of Kloppelgangers (see page 36), and this will only grow in number.

4. Establish the Ministry of Laughter

There's not been a lot to laugh about for some people these last few years – hell, even smiling has been a stretch. It's time to go back to basics. Clowns. Tickling. Dad jokes. A broad sense of joy. You get the picture.

5. Make all eye tests and glasses free at the point of use

When something has served you well, it's healthy to ensure others can benefit from it too. There's nothing to be gained from pulling up the ladder after you. Becoming known as 'the glasses guy' and then opening up the same opportunity to everyone around you? That's just . . . wait for it . . . that's just good optics.

Q: It's one day before the general election, and it's going to be a close-run thing. Your party needs people out on the streets to help get the vote out, but the weather is miserable and you're tempted to stay inside – WWJKD?

A: Turn this into a game: 10 points for getting outside and making it to the meet-up point – that's the most important part, after all. Then one point for every door you knock on, and two for every time you convince someone to switch to your side. Then, at the end of the day, when you're wringing out your soaking-wet clothes, you get a point for every pint glass you can fill with rainwater. The prize for the winner? The pride of knowing you've done the right thing. Oh, and I guess you can also have an evening of not having to pay for a single drink.

THE SECRET TO SUCCESS

Let's imagine Jurgen Klopp has been running a campaign and election night is here. It's time to finally see the results of all that hard work. Jurgen Klopp's platform, of people working for each other, having each other's backs and waging war on the British weather, seems to have caught fire. After all, whatever you say about the British people, moaning about the wind and rain is and always will be a great unifier.

At pubs up and down the country, there are photos of Jurgen Klopp delivering his campaign speeches. People have mocked up the Barack Obama 'Hope' poster with a silhouette of the German's face, because there are only about three good political posters and imagination is overrated. No one is asking why a German is standing for office in a different country because to do so would shatter the suspension of disbelief needed to follow this narrative in the first place. Was that too meta? I'm sorry.

The votes start trickling in. It looks like it's going to be very close. At the halfway point, Klopp's party are trailing and things aren't looking great, but then the later results begin to arrive and it's all in one direction. You can't say he doesn't love an improbable comeback.

As the victory is confirmed, the mood changes from tension to celebration; from hope to disbelief. A chorus of 'You'll Never Walk Alone' breaks out. People are out on the streets rejoicing. It's beautiful.

However impossible something can seem at first, if you think of anything as unwinnable then you don't stand a chance. The first step towards getting something done is convincing *yourself* you can do it. Once you've done that, you'll be surprised by how easily the rest of the pieces fall into place. Winning your five-a-side league. Cooking for 40 people. DJing a club night. It all starts with self-belief.

'There were hard times in the last two years in the EU with Greece, countries in southern Europe really struggling financially, then refugees because of the crisis in Syria. But that's a problem for all people. Let's sort it together'

JURGEN KLOPP, INTERVIEW WITH THE *DAILY TELEGRAPH*, 2018[2]

8. A HOLLYWOOD ENDING

⚽ ⚽ ⚽

JURGEN KLOPP AT THE MOVIES

Think back to the last 10 films you watched. How many were franchise films, and how many were the kind of movie that might be up for an Oscar? And which did you prefer? Be honest.

There are times when you'll be ready for a prestige movie, but you'll need to really be in the right frame of mind to enjoy it. I'm not saying Martin Scorsese was wrong when he argued that superhero blockbusters weren't cinema in the traditional sense – the director made some valid points when he said, 'Many of the elements that define cinema as I know it are there in Marvel pictures. What's not there is revelation, mystery

151

or genuine emotional danger. Nothing is at risk.'[1] Still, the kind of entertainment provided by these movies has a different, yet still valid, function.

This is how we should look at Jurgen Klopp's football teams, too. You get the high stakes of a blockbuster, the presence of something *relatable* at stake which you get in the best prestige cinema, and moments of comic relief and the no-strings-attached enjoyment of children's films. At this point I could try to give you an idea of how Jurgen Klopp's taste in movies can teach you lessons to follow in life, but he's much bigger than that. Klopp has gone far beyond the role of audience member – how could that not be the case when he's so frequently on the other side of the camera? He's a man of complexities you didn't always see coming – like the first time you watched Adam Sandler in a serious drama – who transcends genre but never looks out of place.

If I wanted to really push the children's movie angle, I might say the closest cinematic analogue to Jurgen Klopp is Lots-o'-Huggin' Bear from *Toy Story 3*. After all, the hugging element is right there, staring you in the face. However – spoiler alert – Lots-o' doesn't end up being one of the good guys. (Sorry if I've ruined a classic for you there, but, in my defence, you've had 10 years to catch up.)

You can't liken Klopp to just one film character because, and this is a biggie, films aren't real life. I know, probably a big shock, right? However, while existing characters have their differences, identifying where he fits into the cinematic landscape is easier than you might think. By understanding the cinematic scope of Jurgen Klopp the man and Klopp's football teams, you really can learn a great deal. Maybe you'll even end up surprising yourself.

THE KLOPP FILM FRANCHISE

Jurgen Klopp is a man of many talents, but is he a man of many genres? In short, yes. If you can't imagine him in any of these scenarios, you're simply not thinking hard enough.

• **War Movie Klopp**

Jurgen plays the leader of a down-on-its-luck battalion, part of an army with far fewer resources than its enemy, and at risk of being surrounded from all sides. Through a mixture of motivational speeches and a tactical manoeuvre that no one sees coming, they prevail against all odds. You know, the *Independence Day* kind of speech or the ones that get cited by tech CEOs on LinkedIn when they're trying to sound 'in touch' with culture.

- **Psychological Horror Klopp**

A famous football club is haunted by the spirit of its past and must win a trophy that has eluded them for decades in order to lift the curse. As they draw ever closer to success, their members are struck down in increasingly bizarre and unsettling ways, *Final Destination*-style, but they know they can't afford to take this as a sign. After all, you can never predict when your next opportunity to lift the curse will come along.

- **Marvel Superhero Movie Klopp**

Klopp possesses the range of exaggerated facial expressions you need for a big superhero movie, so he's already got half the job done. He's a Tony Stark type; charismatic and super-intelligent, saving the world from that most common of comic-book tropes, the bald supervillain.[*]

------

[*] Any resemblance to Pep Guardiola is purely coincidental.

- **Spy Thriller Klopp**

A timid pencil-pusher at the CIA needs to ingratiate himself in a foreign city and embrace its customs in order to feed intelligence back to his homeland. He goes undercover as a larger-than-life German football manager, hiding in plain sight and getting so involved in his new persona that he avoids arousing suspicion – even among those closest to him.

- **Kids' Movie Klopp**

After missing his son's big football game, a workaholic father tries to win back the boy's trust by going undercover as the mascot of a school sports team. Throughout the moving final scene, we get the sense that the kid always suspected it was his old man in the costume. Still, the son gets better and better at football on his own, proving he had the talents within him all the time. Can we call this one *Kindergarten Klopp?*

- **Period Drama Klopp**

What's that? You think a perfect British accent is a requisite for this sort of film? Do me a quick favour – go and watch Keanu Reeves in *Bram Stoker's Dracula* and then get back to me.

- **Romantic Comedy Klopp**

This one takes a bit more explaining. Keep reading and I'll reveal more . . .

LIVERPOOL AND JURGEN KLOPP: THE HOTTEST ROMCOM OF THE DECADE

The greatest movie couples all have one thing in common. They have such great chemistry, a rapport so evident to everyone but them, that the two of them ending up together feels inevitable from the first time they meet.

It's not limited to genre, either. For every Harry and Sally there's a Riggs and Murtaugh. For every Cher and Josh, a Schmidt and Jenko. For every Ross and Rachel, a chick and duck.

Jurgen Klopp's relationship with Liverpool is no different. It's part romcom, part buddy cop movie. Or should that be buddy *kop* movie? Allow me to explain.

We begin with the meet-cute. Liverpool had just dumped someone who had given them huge highs and lows over a three-year period, and some thought it was a bad idea to rush into something new. Klopp had come out of a long, passionate relationship too, but he'd taken some time out. He wanted to make sure he didn't still miss Borussia Dortmund, and to guarantee he was ready to fall in love with someone else.

For a while, there was enough tension and questioning to leave us wondering whether it really *was* meant to be. Liverpool finished eighth in the Premier League in Klopp's first season, with some low moments like that 3–0 defeat to Watford and a late, dramatic loss to West Ham in the FA Cup.

We had the unsuccessful finals, the League Cup in 2016, when Manchester City won on penalties. The Europa League the same year, when the excitement of an early Liverpool lead was all for nothing. And then the Champions League in 2018, when everything went wrong with the world watching.

These are moments we all know well, not just in a Liverpool sense but in cinema as a whole. The dramatic peaks and troughs that feel decisive at the time but are just one step along the way. They're the moments we look back on later and chuckle about. Klopp breaks down the fourth wall, pointing out the bits we should be paying close attention to, just in case we got so caught up in the excitement that we missed the ways in which we can follow his lead. You don't always need to push for the grand gesture or the big set piece – sometimes it's about the less showy things, like a well-timed and witty piece of dialogue, or forming genuine human connections. Still, as Klopp's Liverpool showed us against

Barcelona (more on this soon), a big set piece can sometimes be exactly what the moment calls for.

Q: You've taken a trip to the cinema to watch a film you've been desperate to see for weeks, but there's a group of unruly kids behind you, chattering and throwing popcorn. The rest of the theatre is empty so you have no potential allies to call on for help – WWJKD?

A: The only answer is to lean into it. As they throw popcorn, make a show of trying to catch it in your mouth. Latch onto their conversations and join in enthusiastically. Laugh a bit *too* loudly at their jokes. As soon as they realise you're trying to be part of their fun, they'll get bored and give up. You win.

JURGEN KLOPP'S BIGGEST BOX-OFFICE MOMENTS

There aren't a lot of football teams you'd pay to see on the big screen. In fact, there are probably a few you can name who you'd pay good money *not* to see.

It's no coincidence, though, that some of the moments of highest drama involved teams managed by Jurgen Klopp.

Time to book out a screen at your local cinema, invite some friends along, stock up on popcorn and beers and take your pick from these three games. Wondering why I haven't included any league matches? That feels more TV series than big-screen blockbuster, don't you think?

LIVERPOOL 4–3 BORUSSIA DORTMUND, 2015–16 EUROPA LEAGUE

Klopp's first Liverpool season already felt like a bit of a sequel, like Gordon Bombay taking over Team USA after his adventures with the Mighty Ducks. Could he repeat his Dortmund heroics in a new city?

That season had all the hallmarks of a classic Hollywood sports movie. The low point of the dismal European games under Brendan Rodgers. The false dawn of a League Cup final and a penalty shoot-out defeat. And then the Dortmund game.

With 25 of the 180 minutes left in their Europa League quarter-final, Liverpool needed three more goals to go through. All hope was lost.

Then came the turnaround: Philippe Coutinho scored, then Mamadou Sakho left them on the brink. As the board went up for stoppage time, there was Dejan Lovren, the most unlikely hero, to send them through.

Liverpool ended up losing that season's final, but sometimes there are more important things than a Hollywood happy ending.

BORUSSIA DORTMUND 3–2 MALAGA, 2012–13 CHAMPIONS LEAGUE

One thing people often forget about block-busters is that they don't have to be brilliant all the way through. The first leg of Dortmund's game against Malaga was dull. It felt like the teams could have played for days without scoring.

This is why there's often no substitute for watching on the big screen. You might need to wait a while for high drama, but, when it arrives, the pay-off is more than worth it.

With 45 minutes left, Klopp's Dortmund were drawing 1–1 at home and heading out on away goals. With eight minutes remaining, Malaga scored again, leaving Klopp's men needing two. That was still the scenario when the clock ticked past 90 minutes.

But the most dramatic endings come when all hope seems lost at 90+1 minutes: Marco Reus makes it 2–2; 90+3 minutes: Felipe Santana scores the winner. It doesn't matter that the Brazilian was offside – sometimes the rules are no match for the power of narrative.

LIVERPOOL 4–0 BARCELONA, 2018–19 CHAMPIONS LEAGUE

The underdog story dates back to biblical times with David defeating Goliath. That was David v Goliath redux.

Liverpool had lost 3–0 in the first leg. Then they lost Roberto Firmino to injury. Next, Mohamed Salah was stretchered off in a league game.

Liverpool didn't give up. Klopp let them

believe they could win, so they went out believing they could win. They took the lead. But then another injury hit, with Andy Robertson going off at Anfield. This was the moment where the music slows and everything gradually comes into focus. The only way to recover is to treat real life like a movie, and that's what Klopp did.

You need to ride your luck, like the hero dodging a bullet or jumping off a skyscraper to grab hold of a ledge, but you also need to find something original to keep the audience on their toes. Klopp and Liverpool found it. Trent Alexander-Arnold played a quick corner to Divock Origi. Liverpool won. The villain fell to his death. The hero reigned. The credits rolled. The crowd went wild.

'I'm sure everyone will say the 4–0 comeback against Barcelona and the amazing comeback against Dortmund three years earlier are their fondest memories of Klopp. Attacking football, never-say-die attitude, big drama on the grandest stages . . . what more do you want?'

STEVEN CHICKEN

CONCLUSION

⚽ ⚽ ⚽

THE EVOLUTION OF KLOPP

In the time we've known Jurgen Klopp – and it feels like we really do *know* him now – we've watched him morph from a kooky diversion to one of the most important people in English football. Not only that, but for many of us he's become a permanent fixture in our lives. We can mark out our key moments based on where they sit on Jurgen Klopp's arc, and our attachment to him will fit in with how far along we were in our own journeys of self-discovery when he gave us a helping hand along the way.

There might be a temptation to rewrite the past and pretend you let Jurgen Klopp lead the way earlier than he really did. There is no need, though. It's okay to have once been the sort of person who got really into magic tricks for a few months, or decided triple denim was aspirational. You don't need to erase all memory of your past self to prove you're not that person any more.

This applies to learning from Jurgen Klopp the manager but also Jurgen Klopp the man. The point is, people change. People grow. People learn from their past and develop into more well-rounded individuals. Yes, even Jurgen Klopp. Though he could definitely pull off triple denim if he wanted to.

Jurgen Klopp has been a football manager for nearly 20 years. When he started out in the job at Mainz, Facebook didn't exist yet. Atomic Kitten were top of the charts with 'Whole Again'. There was only one *Matrix* film. In short, the world was a very different place to the one we know today.

I'd be surprised if he *hadn't* grown over that period, but it gives hope to the likes of me and you too.

One of the most common tropes in entertainment involves an adult looking back at their younger self.

Sometimes it's the time-capsule concept, where you can speak to yourself across decades (see *Eighth Grade*). Sometimes it's events of the present affecting the past in a weirdly complex butterfly effect (see *Back to the Future* or, well, *The Butterfly Effect*. But you don't need to actually watch the second one). Sometimes it's about being forced to confront your previous self, as in Charles Dickens' *A Christmas Carol* or the infinitely superior *The Muppet Christmas Carol*. Did the original have a character as layered as Fozziwig? That's what I thought. Anyway, I digress.

The main thing to take away from this is that people change a lot over the course of their life, and this applies to you specifically. Yes, you, the person reading this sentence and wondering aloud why I've decided *this* is the moment where I need to break the fourth wall.

When you first got into football, your ignorance was a good thing. It made you open to new experiences, and it allowed you to choose your team using that well-worn scientific method of 'who your dad supported' or 'who the bigger boys at school told you was good'. Occasionally there might be a 'who has a good kit' or 'who has a player with a name I like'. My brother asked for a Liverpool shirt aged six because he liked committing fouls and they had Robbie Fowler up front. Sometimes it actually is that simple.

There really is a point to this, I promise. What we need to bear in mind is that, while we might have stumbled upon some good ideas by dumb luck when we were younger, it's also important to grow and develop into more rounded people. The Jurgen Klopp we know now is not the same man who played for Mainz in his twenties and thirties, and that alone should encourage you and show you that you too can embrace change.

IF YOU DON'T SHOOT, YOU CAN'T SCORE

Jurgen Klopp scored 56 goals in his playing career, but few were as eye-catching as his strike for Mainz against Fortuna Koln in the 1997–98 season. A stunning volley from the right side of the penalty area, it brought back memories of an iconic Marco van Basten goal for the Netherlands nearly a decade earlier. Again, look it up, it really is sensational.

It's the kind of goal we all dreamt of scoring in the school playground, to the point where weekends practising at home turned into weekends ringing your next-door neighbour's doorbell and politely asking if you could come and get your ball back. By the seventh or eighth time of asking, you could see the calm demeanour fade and the cogs move in their head as they determined whether to slam the door in your face.

Still, it was all worth it when the ball fell perfectly for you during the lunchtime 15 v 15 kickabout, the Year 9 v Year 10 *clásico*. Scoring a goal like that gives you kudos. It gives you currency. It gives you something you won't shut up about for years, and anyone *trying* to shut you up will realise that, yeah, OK, you can have this one.

But the Klopp we saw as a player was already well aware of his talents as well as his limitations. If you know you can't drive at speed, you won't get behind the wheel of a Porsche. If you know you're not a numbers guy, you'll make sure your degree requires no maths whatsoever. And if, like Klopp, you see yourself as a better manager than player, you'll make sure you have something left in the tank for later life.

If you're the kind of person who manages a team at work and manages it well, chances are you'll share a few qualities with the big man. He has always been able to blend talented enigmas with strong characters in his squads, finding the right person for each role, and I bet you did the same when hiring someone who might not have been the best individual but was the best fit for your team.

Oh, and when you're watching that clip of Mainz against Wolfsburg from 1997, remember one more thing. He needed a sensational comeback to reach his goal – in this case, promotion to the top flight – and fell just short, but he made sure it would not be his last chance. The arc lasted more than 20 years, not just 90 minutes.

If you fall down on one of your targets, or get some bad news that feels like a punch in the gut, remind yourself there's always time for a comeback. It's never too late. That's what Jurgen Klopp would do.

'We were a real average team, not very well paid, not many people cared about the club but then we learned that even though every single player is better than us we can still beat them – for us, it opened our eyes'

JURGEN KLOPP ON HIS TIME
PLAYING FOR MAINZ[1]

FOLLOW THE PATH THAT'S
RIGHT FOR YOU

Jurgen Klopp isn't the first player to move straight into management, and he won't be the last, but he's set the tone for how the process can and should work.

There's no one path, though. While you can be more like Jurgen Klopp, you don't have to be *exactly* like him. Pep Guardiola was more subdued and less all-action in his time skippering Barcelona. Frank Lampard wasn't even a captain during his playing days at Chelsea. Julian Nagelsmann didn't play a minute of senior professional football before becoming one of Europe's best coaches.

That next great coach? The person who revolutionises the game and has styles of football named after them and popular gift books written about them? They're most likely not even in management yet. There's every chance you haven't even heard of them. Back in 2001, my knowledge of German football was restricted to *Championship Manager* and the occasional Champions League and Uefa Cup match. I barely even knew there *was* a league called 2. Bundesliga. The team name 1. FSV Mainz 05 will have felt alien to me. I might have scrolled past the name 'Jurgen Klopp' while leading my computerised team through pre-season friendlies (if I didn't just 'take a holiday' and leave my assistant in charge), but it wouldn't have stuck in any meaningful sense. That's probably happening with the great manager of the 2030s right now. That manager could even be you, if you really work at it.

Following Jurgen Klopp's lead isn't about doing everything in the same order as him; it's about looking at his journey and picking out the pieces you can replicate. Some people will tell you it's about the journey and not the destination. In truth, it's about both of these things and also about forging your own path. More than a decade passed between Jurgen Klopp's first match as a manager and his first Bundesliga title. If that's not enough of an incentive for you to keep at it and trust the process then, well, are you really asking yourself what Jurgen Klopp would do?

'Boom!'

JURGEN KLOPP

ACKNOWLEDGEMENTS

⚽ ⚽ ⚽

All of this wouldn't have been possible without the help of a lot of great people. First of all, thanks to Ru and everyone at Seven Dials for taking a chance on a football writer whose friends have described him as 'not even one of the better-known clowns'.

To Dan Austin, Steven Chicken, Huw Davies, Grace Robertson and Hari Sethi for sharing your memories and stories, and for those who I spoke to but couldn't find room for. I owe all of you a pint (or can I interest you in one of my range of Klopptails? I have been assured that at least one of them would taste 'potentially OK', and can you really ask for more than that?).

To the Superhunks, for repeatedly shouting 'Write your book' whenever I've started to go off-topic, both on WhatsApp and, somewhat harshly, in person. If it wasn't for your input, I'd probably still be stuck on YouTube watching videos of Borussia Dortmund's 2013 win over Real Madrid instead of actually writing.

To my other group chats, for tactfully and repeatedly shooting down my terrible ideas. Not necessarily ideas related to this book, but my terrible ideas in general. Never stop.

To Brick House and Blackbird Bakery in south-east London, for providing me with coffee, croissants and Wi-Fi and helping me get out of my flat. Yes, I'm 'one of those' writers.

To my parents, who saw me taking an interest in football as a child and decided 'sure, leave him to it, there's no way this will get out of hand'. It's still surreal to me that I get to write about this game for a living.

To all the other family members and friends who have offered support and encouragement along the way, or just told me to shut up when I needed to shut up.

And, finally, to Jurgen Klopp. Thank you for taking that Liverpool job and setting off the chain of events that led to all of this. This one's for you.

NOTES

INTRODUCTION

1 reference for p179 tk
2 Reddy, M., 2017, 'Inside the mind of Jurgen Klopp', https://www.goal.com/story/inside-the-managerial-mind-of-liverpools-jurgen-klopp/index.html; accessed 16 January 2020

1. THE MOST IMPORTANT THING

1 *FourFourTwo*, 2017, 'David Wagner: I can't remember speech at Klopp's wedding – I was too drunk!', https://www.fourfourtwo.com/features/mag-zidanes-quest-why-kaka-snubbed-city-van-der-sar-one-one
2 Davis, C., 2016, 'Brendan Rodgers reveals he invited Jurgen Klopp to his house to help the Liverpool manager

settle in', *The Telegraph*, https://www.telegraph.co.uk/football/2016/02/04/brendan-rodgers-reveals-he-invited-jurgen-klopp-to-his-house-to/; accessed 16 January 2020

3 Pearce, J., 2020, 'Jurgen surprises me every day. His brain works differently to other people', exclusive interview with Klopp's no. 2 Pep Lijnders, *The Athletic,* https://theathletic.com/1513365; accessed 9 January, 2020

4 Renard, A., 2019, 'Liverpool's Pep Lijnders: "Our identity is intensity. It comes back in every drill"', https://www.theguardian.com/football/2019/dec/02/liverpool-pep-lijnders-jurgen-klopp-assistant-paddle-tennis-james-milner; accessed 16 January 2020

2. HUGS AND HANDSHAKES

1 Whalley, M., 2012, 'Sahin Likens Rodgers to Klopp', ESPN, https://www.espn.com/soccer/news/story/_/id/1192286/nuri-sahin-likes-liverpool-boss-brendan-rodgers-to-jurgen-klopp; accessed 9 January 2020

2 Ripley, D., 'Jurgen Klopp says goodbye to Borussia Dortmund fans and hopes to go out with a city centre party following German Cup final', *Daily Mail*, https://www.dailymail.co.uk/sport/football/article-3095992/Jurgen-Klopp-says-goodbye-Borussia-Dortmund-fans-hopes-city-centre-party-following-German-Cup-final.html; accessed 11 January 2020

3 Price, G., 2017, 'Liverpool manager Jurgen Klopp talks transfers, Lucas, Solanke', https://www.espn.co.uk/

football/club/liverpool/364/blog/post/3162138/liverpool-manager-jurgen-klopp-talks-transfers-lucas-solanke; accessed 9 January 2020

3. MENTALITY MONSTERS

1 Torres, D. and Ros, C., 2013, 'Yo no solo quiero ganar; tambien quiero sentir', https://elpais.com/deportes/2013/02/10/actualidad/1360525188_938041.html; accessed 16 January 2020
2 Shaw, C., 2016, 'Jürgen Klopp: That's what I expect from my team', https://www.liverpoolfc.com/news/first-team/235155-jurgen-klopp-that-s-what-i-expect-from-my-team; accessed 11 January 2020
3 reference for p63 tk
4 October 2015, 'Jurgen Klopp interview: Liverpool boss speaks for first time in new role', https://www.independent.co.uk/sport/football/premier-league/jurgen-klopp-interview-liverpool-boss-speaks-for-first-time-in-new-role-a6687336.html; accessed 16 January 2020

4. FOR THE LOVE OF THE GAME

1 https://www.youtube.com/watch?v=MCxTHbZDFFs; accessed 16 January 2020
2 Wahl, G., 2020, 'Jürgen Klopp's Authentic, Infectious Aura and Ultimate Mission', https://www.si.com/soccer/2020/01/16/jurgen-klopp-liverpool-manager-aura-connection; accessed 16 January 2020

5. I LIKE IT LOUD

1 Gotze, M., 2019, 'Danke', https://www.
theplayerstribune.com/en-us/articles/mario-gotze-danke-
dortmund; accessed 16 January 2020

2 Hytner, D., 2013, 'Jürgen Klopp: Borussia Dortmund are
"worth falling in love with"', https://www.theguardian.
com/football/2013/nov/03/borussia-dortmund-jurgen-
klopp-arsenal; accessed 9 January 2020

3 Bascombe, C., 2016, 'Revealed: The secrets behind
Jurgen Klopp's Liverpool', https://www.telegraph.co.uk/
sport/football/teams/liverpool/12101374/Revealed-The-
secrets-behind-Jurgen-Klopps-Liverpool.html; accessed
11 January 2020

4 reference for p104 tk

5 reference for p105 tk

6 reference for p108 tk

7 https://www.youtube.com/watch?v=lZShEy8ILvg

6. THE TASTE OF SUCCESS

1 Gorst, P., 2019, 'Chris Wilder praises Liverpool boss
Jurgen Klopp for being different to other Premier League
managers after post-game drink', *Liverpool Echo*,
https://www.liverpoolecho.co.uk/sport/football/football-
news/chris-wilder-what-jurgen-klopp-17002498; accessed
11 January 2020

2 Reddy, M., 2018, '"I've put everything I have – my

knowledge, passion, heart, experience – into Liverpool'",
https://www.joe.co.uk/sport/jurgen-klopp-interview-
ive-put-everything-i-have-my-knowledge-passion-
heart-experience-into-liverpool-203813; accessed
16 January 2020

7. GETTING YOUR VOTE

1   *DW Kick off!* interview, 2019, https://www.youtube.
com/watch?v=3VSAMrNdIqg&vl=en-GB; accessed 16
January 2020
2   Wallace, S., 2018, 'Jurgen Klopp exclusive interview
on his faith, football, Liverpool future and Brexit',
Daily Telegraph, https://www.telegraph.co.uk/
football/2018/03/30/jurgen-klopp-exclusive-interview-
faith-football-liverpool-future/; accessed 11 January 2020

8. A HOLLYWOOD ENDING

1   https://www.nytimes.com/2019/11/04/opinion/martin-
scorsese-marvel.html.

CONCLUSION

1   Davis, C., 2016, 'Wolfgang Frank: the man who inspired
Jurgen Klopp's coaching philosophy', *Daily Telegraph*,
https://www.telegraph.co.uk/football/2016/09/27/
wolfgang-frank-the-man-who-inspired-jurgen-klopps-
coaching-philo; accessed 9 January 2020

ABOUT THE AUTHOR

TOM VICTOR is a freelance journalist living in London. He writes for Vice, Shortlist, BBC Three, Liverpool.com, Planet Football and more. Mostly about football, but sometimes about pizza and sandwiches.

He thinks about nutmegs and rainbow flicks for about 23 hours of every day.